Casino Marketing

Casino Marketing

Nick Gullo

Published by

Institute for the Study of Gambling
& Commmercial Gaming

Institute for the Study of Gambling
and Commercial Gaming-025
College of Business Administration
University of Nevada, Reno
Reno, NV 89557-0208
PH: 775-784-1442   FX:775-784-1057

ISBN # for Casino Marketing is: 0-942828-47-X.
ISBN # for the Casino Management Series is: 0-942828-45-3.
The Library of Congress Control Number: 2001097031.

Designed by
Trace Publications
325 South 3rd Street 1305
Las Vegas, NV 89101

Printed by
Thomson-Shore, Inc.
Dexter, Michigan

Edited By Rhonda Eade

FOREWORD

This book presents the fundamentals of casino marketing and provides an outline of how a casino can organize its marketing plan. The book covers more than the casino with sections on hotel sales, and room reservations. All major aspects of casino marketing are covered including junkets, special promotions, invited guests, and bus programs. In addition, the reader will learn how to establish a marketing department, prepare a yearly marketing plan and create monthly casino marketing reports. The primary intended audience is casino marketing directors and employees, and casino managers, but this book will serve as a valuable reference for anyone interested in casino marketing.

Casino Marketing is the second in a series of books on casino management published by Institute for the Study of Gambling and Commercial Gaming, College of Business Administration, University of Nevada, Reno. Other books in the series include Casino Math, Casino Credit and Collections, Table Game Management and Slot Machine Management.

This has long been an industry where the amount of written material on casino management has been scarce. This is partially because the audience for such materials has been limited by isolation of casino-style gambling to a few jurisdictions. In the past ten years, this trend has changed dramatically. This also has increased the need for professional casino management materials. The series relies on the collective experience of seasoned casino professionals like Nick Gullo, who have graciously agreed to contribute their time and expertise to the common benefit of the gaming industry.

Anthony N. Cabot
Las Vegas
July 2002

TABLE OF CONTENTS

INTRODUCTION

When Uncle Benny was teaching me to deal, he constantly stressed the importance of learning the basics. He knew that I could not advance my skill level unless I thoroughly understood the basics. If I had a strong foundation, it would prevent me from making costly mistakes in the future. The same philosophy holds true with almost all aspects of life. A solid foundation is necessary to build a house, advance in sports, or achieve any level of expertise in any endeavor or occupation. I would not want a doctor to perform surgery without a solid foundation in medicine and operating procedures! The same applies to casino marketing. Without a thorough understanding of the principles of casino marketing and an in-depth understanding of the basic procedures to follow to reach a goal, a casino executive is doomed to fail.

The foundation of casino marketing lies in understanding its purpose: what it is and why properties need it. Casino marketing is the ability to attract qualified casino customers to a property at a cost that allows the casino to make a profit from their activities. The ability to attract more customers to a property, and to create, and maintain loyalty is imperative.

There is nothing "new" in the world. Some of the basic elements of most things, including casino marketing, look "new," but a closer examination reveals them as "old" with a new name, new look, maybe a new or different process is employed to achieve the same results. The reason the results are the same is because they use the same basic foundation.

This book is a guide to the basics of casino marketing. It is a textbook, but executives who apply the principles of this book will become better equipped to move forward in the world of casino marketing.

Casinos are growing in size; they are now mega-resorts. The casino market has also expanded beyond anyone's futuristic thoughts of ten or even twenty years ago. Various forms of gambling have not only entered every state in the United States except Utah and Hawaii, but we now have cyber-casinos. We have entered the most competitive period in the history of the gaming industry.

We now refer to the gaming industry as entertainment. This is a two-edged sword because we are not only faced with extreme competition within our industry, but we are also challenged with competition from other entertainment venues for the customers' expendable or entertainment dollars. A few examples of this entertainment competition are Disney properties, vacation cruises, sporting events, and many other forms of recreation. Can casinos compete and survive, or even prosper, in the face of this fierce competition? Absolutely! Executives who aggressively market their facilities, and who know how to attract the profitable casino customer will manage successful properties.

A successful casino operator today must maximize profits and manage the property at capacity. Today some casinos place executives in positions for which they do not have the qualifications. They do not know how to bring customers into a casino with a profitable outcome and many new executives are not even clear about what type of customer is right for their property. Top management is not entirely to blame. With so many new casinos and current expansions, talent and experience are being depleted at an alarming rate.

This book gives people currently employed in gaming or those planning to enter the field a solid foundation of a crucial aspect of the industry that before now has been difficult to access other than by trial and error. For example, excellent marketing experts are entering the gaming industry from other fields when they do not understand how to market a casino. Executives are enjoying success as hotel managers, but do not comprehend the marketing aspects of a hotel-casino property. Casinos require certified public accountants to analyze their performance, but some of the accountants do not understand the particular challenges and expenses involved in attracting customers. Regulators, internal auditors, analysts, etc., need to thoroughly understand the management philosophy and costs related to marketing in general, as well as specific marketing events. This book will also benefit casino executives who, over the years have learned the concepts of casino marketing, but want a refresher course.

How confident are casino executives in their ability to properly analyze their property's casino groups, special events, or even the profitability of an individual player? Managers need insight into this phase of casino operations. These same concerns exist outside the casino as well. It is common for people who want to be a casino host to contact casino executives. They sincerely want to start a business relationship with the casino, either as an outside agent or a company employee (host) but do not understand the most basic questions about the type of customers the casino wants to attract.

Students studying Hotel Administration also need more exposure to the basic elements of a casino marketing program. Even players who expect the casino to comp (grant a complimentary) them should understand casino marketing to have a better understanding of their own situation.

Most things in life come full circle, and as such, competition will continue to increase. Aggressive marketing executives have the opportunity to increase the bottom-line profit of a casino by using gambling junkets, but they must have a thorough understanding of this segment of the market. A chapter of this book is devoted to the discussion of junkets.

Recently an executive from a large property who wanted to discuss the feasibility of a junket program approached me. He wanted to attract more casino-oriented customers to his property and was exploring this market segment. He recognized the profit potential of a well-managed junket program and was wise enough to do his homework before he made commitments.

Potential representatives may know many players, but they must also know how many to bring in at one time and the right days and times to bring them to the property. The representative, the player, and the casino executive should also know exactly what players must do once they are in the casino. As basic as these issues are, many aspiring representatives and young casino executives do not know how to handle them.

Special events are the sizzle on the steak of casino marketing; they are the enticement or the "carrot at the end of the stick" for the casino customer. Everyone wants a comp ticket to a major championship fight, a ticket to the super bowl or World Series, or to attend the special gala or extravagant New Year's Eve party. The hotel-casino does not always make a profit from these special events, but not by design. The sad part is that quite often special events are incorrectly planned and consequently result in a disappointment for the property both financially and in terms of customer satisfaction.

Would you know how to evaluate the potential of a special event for your property? Would you know how to coordinate an event that top management would embrace? People who think casinos are bottomless pits of wealth or who are unconcerned about a profitable bottom line sometimes bombard casino executives with ideas, plans, and schemes. A casino executive needs to understand how to evaluate each event on an individual basis and assess how the event fits into the property's overall marketing plan and schedule.

Seasoned casino executives understand the value of a good special event segment of their marketing strategy and constantly search for profitable special events. Many times a property looks for ways to make an idea work because it has a benefit to the community, but they must also understand the cost to either make it profitable or to minimize the loss. Once employees understand this aspect of casino marketing, they will stop assuming casinos have an unlimited flow of cash and begin to consider the profit line.

Many other professionals are also indirectly pulled into the casino arena. Politicians at all levels consistently encounter difficult questions about casino operations and casino marketing. As they begin to understand how casino marketing functions and as they become more sophisticated in their analysis skills, answers to their questions will come more easily.

Marketing executives from other industries are jumping into the gaming industry, but casinos have a strong siren song for corporate executives unfamiliar with gaming operations. Without the proper understanding of how to attract customers and develop loyalty, executives will fling themselves perilously into career disaster. This book explains the many different markets available to a property and how to incorporate them into the company's marketing strategy. Managers will also learn how to analyze and develop the optimum marketing mix for a particular property. This book demonstrates how to analyze each market and the segment of each of those markets. It shows casinos how to protect themselves from costly mistakes by pre-planning and pre-analyzing every segment of the market brought to the property and how to analyze the value of each customer.

CHAPTER 1: MARKETING MIX

Chapter Outline

Marketing Mix Definition

Marketing Departments
- Sales Department
- Room Reservations Department
- Casino Marketing Department

Property Analysis
- Physical Facilities
- Financial Requirements
- Personnel

Cost of Marketing

MARKETING MIX

The most profitable situation in the marketing of a hotel/casino operation is for the casino alone to fill all of the rooms, seven days a week, with qualified casino customers.

If you have a property with 1,000 rooms--which by today's standards is not a large property--it is physically impossible for the casino to utilize all of the rooms on a daily basis at a profit. In a 30-day month, a 1,000-room hotel has to fill 30,000 room nights. A casino alone and its support areas could not service the number of guests necessary to fill this number of rooms at a profit. A casino can only provide quality service to a limited number of customers at one time. Therefore, to keep the hotel rooms occupied, other sources of business must occupy some rooms. This is vital to the success of the property because nothing is more perishable than a hotel room night. When allowed to remain empty, the revenue lost one night from the empty room cannot be retrieved.

These various business sources are commonly referred to as the Marketing Mix. Departments that specialize in selling and handling the various business sources are often responsible for bringing in the mix. Together these departments achieve the desired occupancy necessary to produce a bottom-line profit.

MARKETING DEPARTMENTS

These departments usually can be categorized into the following areas:

1. Hotel Sales Department
2. Room Reservations Department
3. Casino Marketing Department

Each of these departments is required, through a formal sales plan, to produce a percentage of the total occupancy of the hotel. The following table is an example of a very simple Marketing Mix for a 1,000-room hotel.

Table 1.1 Marketing Mix

Area	Percentage of Occupancy	Room Nights
Sales Department	40%	12,000
Room Reservations	40%	12,000
Casino Marketing	20%	6,000
Totals	**100%**	**30,000**

Room nights refer to the total rooms available to rent by a hotel, multiplied by the number of nights in the month. The 1,000-room hotel we will use as the model throughout this book would therefore have 30,000 room nights available in a 30-day (night) period.

A Sales Department's main function is to sell hotel rooms to non-casino oriented groups. These groups are comprised of various types of conventions, incentive groups, tour and travel groups, and tour wholesalers. The Sales Department wants these hotel guests to play in the casino but the primary objective of these groups is to provide the hotel with room, food and beverage revenues.

Room Reservations is responsible for selling the hotel rooms to individuals or small groups (usually less than 10 people but this number will vary according to hotel policy) as a pre-arrival reservation or on a walk-in basis. This department also handles special hotel package sales to individuals through travel agents or through special advertising campaigns or promotional ads.

The Room Reservations Manager's responsibilities include coordinating room usage through various sales departments and individuals. This Manager must insure the hotel maintains a pre-determined occupancy level without "overbooking," thereby causing some guests to be "walked" or turned down when they arrive at the hotel front desk to register. It would waste valuable time and money and be a serious problem for the Sales Department to sell to a group requiring 80 rooms on a specific date when they only have 50 rooms available for sale.

Casino Marketing is responsible to bring customers to the property whose primary desire is to gamble in the casino. These customers are usually extended, on some level, complimentary room, food, and beverage privileges, based on the amount of action they generate in the casino. Their importance is based on the premise that casino customers produce more revenue in a shorter time period than other types of customers. Therefore, the property gives this department priority on the number of rooms, banquet, and meeting room facilities needed to accommodate its customers.

Accordingly, if the hotel finds itself "overbooked," then naturally they accommodate the casino customer first. Careful consideration must be given when granting this priority privilege to the Casino Marketing Department so that it does not continually take hotel rooms away from the Sales Department, preventing that area from reaching its marketing objectives and revenue goals. This pitfall will prove disastrous to your overall, long-range marketing strategy.

PROPERTY ANALYSIS

An important aspect in developing a proper Marketing Mix for a hotel/casino operation is an understanding of the property itself. Recognizing its advantages and shortcomings is an extremely important step to determine the right Marketing Mix. Managers must carefully consider the physical attributes and deficiencies of the hotel/casino, the financial position, and requirements of the property, and even the type of personnel who staff the property and service the customers.

The Excalibur, the Las Vegas Hilton, and Caesars Palace are three classic examples in Las Vegas. The physical facilities of Excalibur are attractive to the family traveler. The Las Vegas Hilton is located next to the Las Vegas Convention Center, and the hotel itself has some of the finest convention facilities of any hotel in the world. Therefore, an important and large segment of its business comes from conventions. Caesars Palace is one of the most beautiful, luxurious hotels in the world, and as a result, attracts the "high roller" casino guest.

Executives cannot over emphasize the importance of understanding the type of property they have to market, and then to consistently move in that direction. Many hotels have failed because their executives did not properly define the potential markets available to their property based on an honest evaluation of their physical facilities. They can also fail to "stay on course" once the direction is determined. One common error (and a sad one) is for a middle-market property to pursue the extreme high roller market without having the physical facilities or the personnel to compete with the ultra-luxury hotel/casinos.

Some properties have been very successful from a bottom-line standpoint because they marketed to the $5,000 to $10,000 credit-line casino customer. As time progressed, management began to make stronger gaming demands on the customers by raising the minimum betting criteria in the casino, and at the same time extending fewer incentives to the customers. Consequently, they lost their regular "repeat" customers without having the physical facility to attract the $10,000 to $25,000 credit line casino customer. These casinos then found themselves without a broad enough base of regular customers from which to draw. When this happens, it usually becomes the beginning of the end because in a short period the sales efforts of all the departments start to continually change direction. This leads to wasting money and time on emergency, short-range plans. The property flounders because it suffers from a lack of image and direction.

Consider for a minute the pyramid theory of building your market. You must build a base of one level of business broad enough and strong enough in terms of quantity and quality, before you pursue a higher and more limited class of business. You can balance various markets on a smaller basis for a time, but when the wind blows--such as tough economic times, an airline strike, etc., and you have not yet built a broad, regular, and loyal base of business, you will have to scamper for short-term business that usually grows more expensive and less profitable. Make certain that your property can physically accommodate the new and/or additional clientele you seek. For example, it would be fruitless to pursue conventions rather than individual tours without having adequate meeting rooms. It could prove fatal to pursue the high roller market without having an adequate number of hotel suites and several first-class dining facilities.

At Caesars Palace, for instance, some of the suites are exquisitely decorated, split-level areas furnished with everything the guest could desire, including grand pianos. The Desert Inn had suites with private swimming pools. These suites were, as one might guess, reserved for the more lucrative casino customers.

To attract the caliber of customer to a property that has only one-bedroom suites to offer would be difficult. This does not mean a smaller property should never invite a potential high roller as a houseguest or to dine in the gourmet room. However, the management team of a smaller property should never structure its marketing plans with the main emphasis on the pursuit of this level of player.

Sometimes pursuing the high-level casino customer because of the financial condition of the property is necessary. Casino executives occasionally find their property experiencing negative cash flow, and consequently, must pursue higher-level customers to generate quick revenue to service its debt structure. When you are in a position where you have obtained the normal and proper marketing mix for your property, and you still operate at a loss, then you have no choice but to aggressively pursue high-level customers. If you find yourself in this situation or one similar to it, make certain you have a marketing department comprised of aggressive, hard-working, astute executives who know how to attract the right customers into the casino. At this point, you have no choice but to over-emphasize your marketing strategies, both in terms of effort and monetary expenditures in the areas of advertising, special promotions, and offering additional incentives for the customers.

A successful casino must have knowledgeable personnel who have appropriate skills to accommodate the type of customers they need to attract to the property. Executives must have the ability, both verbally and through their actions, to deal with the customers in a polite and dignified manner, and in a way that lets the customers know their patronage is important. Quite often a good employee with many years of successful casino experience gets promoted to a position where they are suddenly removed from behind the gaming tables to a position where they are required to service the customers' daily needs and requests. If the executives are unable to adjust to their new roles, the casino should move them back to positions where they can make a contribution to the operation rather than unknowingly encumber the marketing efforts.

COST OF MARKETING

Some executives feel they are "buying business" when they make payments directly to the customer in the form of reimbursement of airfare and/or complimentary room, food and beverage privileges. However, any time you create an expense in an effort to attract customers to your property, you are to some extent buying business. If, in the pursuit of the individual tourist, you purchase advertisements in travel industry magazines, highway billboards, or radio commercials, you are creating an expenditure that you must deduct from the revenue. Therefore, you have purchased the business.

You need to carefully examine and coordinate your Advertising and Sales Department expenditures with the various segments of the market you are pursuing. For example, you would not want to spend 25% of your advertising budget to pursue the "package customer" if that category of customer will represent only 5% of your overall occupancy or revenue. You also would be equally remiss to send sales representatives on costly trips in pursuit of business that only represents a small segment of your overall business.

Regardless of what type of business you pursue and/or attain it must be "purchased" through attendance at sales conventions, by members of your sales staff, or by direct incentives given to the customers. Do not be afraid to "buy" business, but make certain you receive value and profit for what you've "purchased." You must maintain a balance between expenditures and results.

CHAPTER 2: HOTEL SALES

Chapter Outline

Objective of a Sales Department

Sales Department

Sales Department Components
     Citywide Conventions
     In-house Conventions
     Incentive Groups
     Tour and Travel Groups
     Wholesale Travel

OBJECTIVE OF A SALES DEPARTMENT

The main objective of a Sales Department is to sell hotel rooms to non-casino groups in conformity with the guidelines set forth in your current year's Sales Plan. The Sales Plan for the property is the guiding light that determines what type of business, and how much of each type of business the Sales Department will try to bring to the property during the year.

A Sales Department is generally made up of a Director of Sales, a Sales Manager, a Tour and Travel Department Coordinator, Convention Coordinator and an Incentive Group Coordinator. The Director of Sales has the responsibility to assist the General Manager and other marketing executives in formulating the over-all Sales Plan. The Director of Sales is then totally responsible for the success of the Sales Department in achieving the goals set forth in the Sales Plan. This person hires and supervises all of the personnel within the Sales Department, and ensures that the efforts of the Sales Department personnel coordinate with that of the other Marketing Departments and Food and Beverage Department pertaining to convention banquets and luncheons.

In a 1,000-room property (or larger), executives will find it necessary to divide the Sales Department into sub-departments, or areas of specialization. One such "sub" department might specialize in selling the hotel to convention groups. Within this area you should designate a salesperson as a convention coordinator. The convention coordinator's responsibility is to work with the convention groups to provide all the services they will need to make their convention successful. The convention coordinator also works with the Food and Beverage Department to secure all the food items the groups need for meetings, lunches, and/or banquets.

The salesperson who originally booked the convention for the hotel is responsible for meeting with the room reservations manager to coordinate the number and type of rooms necessary, the arrival and departure dates of the guests, and all pertinent information regarding the financial aspects of the group.

The Tour and Travel Department's responsibilities include selling a portion of the hotel according to the sales plan to travel agents and tour wholesalers in blocks of 10 or more rooms. For the Tour and Travel Department to accomplish its goals, its representatives must work with tour and travel agencies throughout the world on a daily basis to build friendships and a rapport with the tour operators.

A Tour and Travel Department Director has the responsibility of working with the Room Reservations Manager to coordinate the business he has sold for the hotel. The responsibilities of the Tour and Travel Director include coordinating the names of the guests arriving on the tour, arrival and departure dates, the amenities included in their "package," and the financial arrangements for the group.

The organization of a Sales Department depends on several variables: the types of group business the hotel sells, the talents of the various individuals working within the Sales Department. For example, one person may be able to cover two or more areas.

The Director of Sales is responsible for properly structuring the organizational chart to maximize the talents of the people within the department. The Director of Sales should continually evaluate and measure the performance of each salesperson and be prepared to make changes and assignments to motivate the sales staff. Through trade shows, sales trips, Travel Agent familiarization trips, and other such endeavors, a sales department has many opportunities to network for potential employees or to pursue new markets.

SALES DEPARTMENT – MARKETING MIX

The Marketing Mix of the Sales Department can be categorized into the following five areas:

- Citywide Conventions
- In-House Conventions
- Incentive Groups
- Tour and Travel Groups
- Tour Wholesalers

The previous theoretical example of a 1,000-room hotel, shows the Sales Department's responsibility for selling 40% of the rooms, or 12,000 room nights per month. With this guideline in mind, a suggested marketing mix objective for the Sales Department can be found in Table 2.1. Keep in mind this is only a theoretical example of one possible marketing mix. Your sales plan and ultimately your marketing mix is determined only after giving careful consideration to the saleable attributes of your particular property and the markets available.

Table 2.1 Marketing Mix Objective - Sales Department

Area	Percentage	Room Nights
Citywide Conventions	2%	600
In-House Conventions	6%	2,400
Incentive Groups	20%	6,000
Tour and Travel Groups	5%	1,500
Tour Wholesaler	5%	1,500
Total	**40%**	**12,000**

Citywide Conventions

A citywide convention originates through the City Convention Authority or Bureau. In a citywide convention, conventioneers are housed in at least three different hotels. Citywide conventions usually hold their main meetings and other functions at a city convention center rather than at the individual hotels. Conventions of this nature are important to the economic well being of a city and to the hotels in which the convention delegates stay. This isn't the most lucrative market for the individual hotel because of the limited number of functions held within the hotel, and because the hotel usually charges only a group-discounted room rate. Because conventions are not the most profitable form of business for the hotels, many properties elect to support the convention center and the city in general by not providing rooms for these types of groups at a convention rate.

The Homebuilders Association's annual convention, for example, is one of the world's largest conventions and is highly sought after by convention cities throughout the world because of its tremendous positive financial impact on the host city. However, because of the huge number of delegates attending this convention, and the large and numerous exhibits on display, it is necessary to hold most of its meetings, functions and exhibits in a large, citywide convention facility.

In-House Conventions

In-house conventions are pursued by the hotel's Sales Department primarily because of revenue from room sales, meeting facilities, and food and beverage functions, such as banquets and breakfast meetings. These conventions are usually confined to one industry at a time, such as physicians' seminars, attorneys' workshops, associations for a common product (such as the National Auto Parts Association-NAPA), or other special interest or hobby groups. In-house conventions are very lucrative for a hotel, not only because of the large number of food and beverage functions they book in the host hotel, but because of the money attendees spend when they finish their work for the day.

Incentive Groups

Incentive Groups are the most lucrative groups the Sales Department can bring to a hotel-casino property. Incentive groups are brought to the hotel, usually by their company, as a reward to employees for achieving goals or meeting quotas. These companies also hold high-level conferences and meetings. The company usually requests the better rooms, and pay prevailing rates. These companies spare no expense when it comes to their banquets, meetings, and cocktail parties. The most important element that makes this type of business the most profitable for a hotel-casino property, is that the company pays for all of the attendees' expenses. Therefore, they have more spendable pocket money for the casino and other recreational activities, such as shows and gourmet dining. The attendees at an incentive-type meeting usually rank high in the company, and, for that reason have more disposable income.

Because of the benefits this caliber of group has at a property, managers should emphasize the sales efforts in this direction. However, this is one situation where a hotel is able to attain quality of guests, but not quantity. It is, unfortunately, a limited market.

When pursuing any type of convention business, including incentive groups, consideration must be given to the physical requirements of the groups prior to spending the time, money, and effort in pursuing their business. For example, it would not be appropriate to attract one of the major automobile manufacturers to a property to introduce their new models if the hotel does not have a convention room large enough to display the vehicles.

Tour and Travel Groups

Tour and Travel Groups are groups that utilize 10 or more rooms sent to the property by a Travel Agent on a net room basis. If the Travel Agent makes reservations for less than 10 rooms, Room Reservations generally handles it on an individual basis (The number of rooms designated as a group varies according to each property's policy). This type of business is usually sold in a package, which consists of a room (single or double occupancy), specially priced meals, shows, drinks, transfers to and from the airport, baggage handling and various other amenities.

Travel groups are not the most lucrative form of business because the various components that make up the package are sold at a discounted rate. Sales Representatives who specialize in dealing with Travel Agents pursue the Tour and Travel Group market. By attending the various Tour and Travel Agents' trade shows held throughout the United States, and by heavy advertising in the magazines and catalogs that cater to this industry, such as *Travel Trade Magazine* and *Travel Weekly*, Sales Representatives can have an edge on this market.

When pursuing tour and travel groups, creating a competitive package in both price and amenities is important. If your property does not have the physical facilities to compete with the other nearby hotels for large business, consider a price reduction to make your package attractive. Any property can design a marketable package if you, as the hotel executive, are realistic in appraising the price of your package in comparison to the competition. This type of business is more quantity than quality, and the only thing that limits the amount of business you pursue in this area is the profit margin generated by the market.

Tour Wholesalers

A Tour Wholesaler is a large tour company that sells hotel rooms to many retail travel agents at a wholesale rate. The wholesaler "blocks" a large number of rooms on a set pattern--some "block" rooms seven days a week, others, on certain days of the week. This is the least lucrative business that a hotel generates due to the low room rate given to the tour wholesaler in return for the guarantee to buy the agreed-upon number of rooms. The attractive aspect of this market is that you can depend on having a predetermined occupancy level, even during your hotel's seasonal slow periods. The volume of people also increases revenues in other areas, such as restaurants, casinos and shops.

In a package tour by a wholesaler, the customer receives a discounted package, which includes reduced airfare, reduced hotel room rate, transfers to and from the hotel, baggage handling, and various other amenities. Travel through the tour wholesaler is generally the least expensive way for an individual to travel, but the traveler must take his trip with a group and can only travel on certain days and at certain times. In essence, the individual traveler receives a monetary discount, but loses the flexibility in scheduling desired arrival and departure times, and choices of accommodations.

Tour wholesalers usually achieve lower air transportation costs using air charter equipment, or by committing to a pre-determined number of seats on a regular schedule, through a particular airline.

From a hotel's standpoint, it is important to closely monitor a tour wholesaler's room blocks so the hotel has the necessary time to sell canceled rooms. They must also closely scrutinize payment procedures.

CHAPTER 3: ROOM RESERVATIONS

Chapter Outline

Objective of Room Reservations

Room Reservations Department

Room Reservations
> Individuals
> Packages
> Walk-ins

OBJECTIVE OF ROOM RESERVATIONS

The Room Reservations Department is responsible for selling hotel rooms to individual guests or to travel agents who make reservations for individual guests. If the Room Reservations Department receives an inquiry for 10 or more rooms, it usually turns this request over to the Sales Department which will handle this business as a group.

An experienced Room Reservations Manager with a staff of Room Reservations Clerks usually oversees a Room Reservations Department. The number of clerks in this department varies according to the size of the hotel. A Room Reservations Manager needs a great deal of experience because of the responsibility of making on-the-spot decisions whether or not to accept or reject individual reservations. They also need to know when to save rooms for both the casino and the Sales Department. At the same time, they must book enough rooms by individual reservations to obtain a good occupancy and room revenue level.

A capable, experienced Room Reservations Manager is an extremely important ingredient in the Sales-Team of a property. The Room Reservations Manager has the responsibility of keeping everyone, especially the various Sales Departments, informed of the number of rooms available for sale on any given day. This manager is also responsible for keeping the Casino Marketing Department, the Sales Department, and Hotel Management informed of the percentage of rooms booked with the various types of businesses, and the overall occupancy.

The Room Reservations Manager also has the responsibility to prepare a Daily Occupancy Report. This report shows the number of rooms that were available, the number of rooms that were occupied (sold or comped), the average dollar rate that was charged for each room, and several other key factors that deal with the occupancy of the hotel. The Occupancy Report is important to sales departments and management because it gives a daily breakdown of the business and room revenues that actually occurred, rather than just a forecast. This report should also include a month-to-date column and a column to compare the activities for the same period in the previous year-to-date. The Room Reservations Manager is also responsible for preparing a weekly cap of the business the hotel actually handled, compared to its occupancy and revenue projections, and a forecast for the following week.

Figure 3.1 Daily Occupancy Report

Date:

By:

ROOM REVENUE	TODAY	M.T.D	L.MT.D.	Y.T.D
Casino Comps	$11,000	$165,000	$170,500	$3,795,000
Bus Comps	250	3,500	3,875	86,250
Other Comps	0	275	330	6,050
Casino Rates	625	8,750	8,500	26,250
Groups	12,800	187,520	189,120	4,143,400
Walk-Ins	1,750	25,725	23,625	595,350
Package	2,700	35,775	36,720	837,675
Others	5,250	73,500	71,400	1,792,000
TOTAL ROOM REVENUE:	$34,375	$500,045	$504,070	$11,272,975
ROOMS AVAILABLE:	1000	15,000	15,000	345,000
ROOMS OCCUPIED:				
Casino Comps	200	3,000	3,100	69,000
Bus Comps	10	140	155	3,450
Other Comps	0	5	6	110
Casino Rates	25	350	340	1,050
Groups	400	5,860	5,910	129,200
Walk-Ins	50	735	675	17,010
Package	100	1,325	1,360	31,025
Others	150	2,100	2,040	51,200
TOTAL ROOMS OCCUPIED:	935	13,515	13,586	302,045
OCCUPANCY PERCENTAGE:	93.5%	90.1%	90.6%	87.6%
ROOM AVERAGE RATE:	$36.76	$37.00	$37.10	$37.32
CASINO NO-SHOWS:	2	29	24	327
NO-SHOWS WITH DEPOSITS:	5	63	58	1,016
REVENUE FROM NO-SHOWS:	$175	$2,205	$2,030	$35,560
OUT OF ORDER ROOMS:	0	0	0	0

Figure 3.2 Weekly Occupancy Report

Rooms	Monday		Tuesday		Wednesday		Thursday		Friday		Saturday		Sunday	
	Proj	Act	Proj	Act	Proj	Act	Proj	Act	Proj	Act	Proj	Act	Proj	A
Available	1000	1000	1000	1000	1000	1000	1000	1000	1000	1000	1000	1000	1000	100
Rented	900	890	900	870	950	970	960	980	1000	1000	1000	1000	825	8
Occupancy %	90	89	90	87	95	97	96	98	100	100	100	100	82.5	8
Average Rate	$35	$36	$35	$36	$32	$31	$32	$31	$44	$46	$44	$45	$35	$3

Note: This report is to be prepared and submitted to th Executive Office by 8:00 PM Sunday evening. Tw reports will be submitted each week. The first report w provide the projected occupancy for the upcoming weel The following report will include the actual occupanc report on a copy of the initial report. At that time, you w submit the Occupancy Report for the following week.

Recap for the Week:

Rooms	Projected	Actual
Available	7,000	7,000
Rented	6,535	6,510
Occupancy %	93.36	93.0
Average Rate	$36.88	$37.18
Total Revenue	$240,995	$242,010

Report prepared by: _____

Room Reservations Manager

Date: _____

Figure 3.3 Monthly Occupancy Report (2000)

	JAN	FEB	MAR	APR	MAY
ROOMS AVAILABLE	31,000	28,000	31,000	30,000	31,000
ROOMS RENTED	27,760	23,265	28,640	29,300	29,450
OCCUPANCY	96.0%	83.1%	92.4%	97.7%	95.0%
AVG. ROOM REVENUE	$36.00	$35.00	$37.00	$36.50	$36.00
TOTAL REVENUE	$1,071,360	$823,581	$1,059,680	$1,069,450	$1,060,200

Note: This report is to be prepared and submitted to the Executive Office on the first day of the month.

ROOM RESERVATIONS DEPARTMENT--MARKETING MIX

The Room Reservations Department handles three basic types of business:

1. Individuals: Guests make their reservations directly with the hotel or through a travel agent prior to arriving.

2. Packages: An advertised package usually consists of a room (single or double occupancy), several meals, a show, transfers to and from the airport, and baggage handling in and out of the hotel. Guests are usually aware of this package through advertisements in newspapers, magazines or through a Travel Agent.

3. Walk-ins: Guests who simply walk into a hotel and request a hotel room at the prevailing rate.

The majority of business that comes through the Room Reservations Department is secured by the use of the various advertising media, which is directed both to the guests and to the travel agent.

The Room Reservations Department's efforts and expertise plays a crucial role in obtaining the desired occupancy and revenue level necessary to produce a bottom-line profit because this department usually accounts for approximately 40% of the hotel's occupancy. The Room Reservations Department is the unsung hero of the sales efforts of practically every major hotel. If a department produces 40% of a hotel's sales results, it would behoove members of top management to take the time to get to know the salespeople.

CHAPTER 4: CASINO MARKETING

Chapter Outline

OBJECTIVE OF CASINO MARKETING

The Casino Marketing Department has the responsibility of attracting casino-oriented customers to the hotel/casino in conformity with the overall marketing plan of the property. The Director of Casino Marketing heads this department. He or she, along with other members of top management, has the responsibility to identify the salable qualities of the property and the different types of markets to attract.

When the marketing mix of a casino is identified, it is essential to assemble the appropriate personnel for the department. For example, the casino should select someone with a congenial personality to handle invited guests, and someone with administrative abilities should handle special promotions. Choosing the best personnel available for each area of the Casino Marketing Department is critical, because this department is expected to generate the largest portion of the property's revenue and profit.

The Director of Casino Marketing also has the responsibility to coordinate the activities of the Hotel Sales Department, Room Reservations, and the Casino Marketing Departments. This coordination is the key to a harmonious and unified sales effort by all Sales Departments and is necessary to maintain a high level of occupancy, and to produce the best possible casino, room, food and beverage revenue per occupied room.

Because the Casino Marketing Department personnel bring casino customers to the property, they must maintain a close working relationship with the staff of the casino. Having key members of this department with casino experience is a definite advantage.

The profit structure of the hotel/casino depends on having a sufficient number of room nights used by qualified casino customers to generate the necessary casino action to allow the property to produce a net bottom-line profit.

Properties attract customers by having a combination of programs for different levels and sources of guests. These different programs make up a "Casino Marketing Mix." The Marketing Mix for almost all casino properties can be broken down into the following five areas:

- Junkets
- Special Promotions
- Invited Guests
- Casino Rate
- Bus Customers

Using our 1,000-room hotel as the example, a possible 30-day Marketing Mix would be as follows:

Table 4.1 Casino Marketing Mix

Area	Percentage	Room Nights
Junkets	8%	2,400
Special Promotions	1%	300
Casino Rate	1%	300
Invited Guests	10%	3,000
Bus Customers	0	0
Total	**20%**	**6,000**

For the sake of clarity, following is a brief description of each area of casino business mentioned in the above marketing mix breakdown. A complete analysis of each area of casino business is made in later chapters.

JUNKETS

A junket is a group of individuals that usually totals eight or more, which is sent or brought to the casino by one of its representatives for the purpose of gambling. The representative brings the players from a specific geographic area and the casino pays a commission per qualified player, or is on a yearly salary. If the players meet the criteria established by the casino, they receive complimentary room, food, beverage, and airfare privileges, or a combination thereof.

The overall cost per player of a junket is actually less than the cost per player of the customers brought into the casino by a Casino Host, because the junket representative can acquire group air rates or charter an aircraft, and usually encourages the customer to play more in the casino to qualify as a VIP customer. A well-managed junket program could easily provide you with 2,400 room nights per month, with approximately 700 room nights or 30% of the program consisting of individual customer send-ins by your junket representative.

SPECIAL PROMOTIONS

A casino special promotion is any event used to attract a casino customer to your property.

Most special promotions can be classified into two categories:

- ▶ In-house promotions (active); and
- ▶ Outside promotions (inactive).

In-house promotions are events that you create for your casino customers, (e.g. golf tournaments, tennis tournaments, and prizefights). Most casino properties should have enough casino customers to host a major event (200 customers) each quarter, and a small event (25 to 50 customers) each month.

Outside promotions take place at another casino's property. You invite your casino customers to stay with you, and they participate in the other property's events. Examples of such events are prizefights held at another hotel, charity golf tournaments hosted by a local civic club, or a nearby (within a few hundred miles) Super Bowl, World Series, Olympics, or other such events. Properly managed special promotions can be profitable, but expensive. If they are not carefully managed and controlled, special events can result in heavy financial losses. Special promotions are discussed in detail in chapter 6.

INVITED GUESTS

Invited Guests are players who come to your property because they are friends of, or know a casino executive or Casino Host, or because they simply like the physical amenities your property has to offer. Most casinos that cater to premium casino customers do so through the use of executives, whose main function is to invite known casino customers to their casino, and to service (take care of; cater to) said guests when they arrive.

CASINO RATE

Casino Rate is a special discount on the price of the guest's hotel room. Casinos give this special discount to customers who do not play to a high enough limit in the casino to warrant a free room or other complimentary privileges. Quite often, you will extend this reduced room rate to a friend or relative of a "high roller" player who asks you to do something special for a friend as a favor.

BUS PROGRAM

A bus program is normally designed to attract slot machine players and value-conscious casino customers to your casino. A bus program has a definite value to a hotel/casino property because it brings casino-oriented customers to the property without those customers occupying rooms. The obvious advantage of this situation is that it allows you to have both casino customers and hotel customers, an extremely important aspect for a property with a limited number of rooms.

EVALUATING CASINO PLAYERS

To have an effective and profitable Casino Marketing Program of any type, you must invite qualified casino customers to your property, and to extend complimentary privileges to them according to their casino action, on a trip-by-trip basis.

Who is a qualified player? How much can you afford to pay for a player's business? Due to the spiraling expenses involved in bringing a customer to your property, it is extremely important to make sure that you have a chance to win a sufficient amount from this player to overcome the promotional costs. These costs can include paying for airfare for the player and a guest (commonly referred to as Mr. & Mrs. Airfare), giving a complimentary room, food and beverage during their stay, extending casino credit, and at times, the additional expenses involved in hosting a special event

Your earning potential from each player is determined by three factors:

- ► How much money the player has in cash, credit or both.
- ► How much the player is willing to wager on each bet.
- ► How long of a period the player is willing to play.

Now that you know what to look for from players to determine if their casino action warrants giving them complimentary privileges, how do you know if they are in fact, playing in the casino, and to what extent? It's simple-- watch all players and record every play they make in the casino. It is not as difficult as you (and the players) might imagine.

Player Rating Slip

Every time players go to a gaming table, the casino floorperson (in the gaming pit) identifies them and prepares a rating slip on their play. This is not a difficult task. The following sample takes you through each step in preparing a rating slip just as the casino floorperson would complete the form.

Figure 4.1a Player Rating Slip (blank)

Date_____D___S____G_____

Name_____

Credit Line_____FM_____

Reg_____Junket_____

Dice_____BJ_____Roul_____

1ST BET	INDIVIDUAL MARKERS TAKEN
Average	
Bet	

WON_____LOST_____

TIME IN_____TOT_____

TIME

_____

REMARKS: initials:

Figure 4.1b Player Rating Slip (completed)

Date 12/15   D X   S_____G_____

Name John Smith_____

Credit Line 5,000   FM_____

Reg_____Junket New York_____

Dice_____BJ_____Roul_____

1ST BET	INDIVIDUAL MARKERS TAKEN
25	500
Average	
Bet	
60	

WON_____ LOST - 200

TIME IN 1:15 TOT 2 ¼

TIME

_____

REMARKS: initials: N.G.

Bets.Propositions

In this sample, on December 15, the player, Mr. John Smith, came to dice table #2 during the day shift and requested a $500 marker. When he presented the proper identification, the casino floorperson checked his credit, then gave him $500 in chips to start playing on table #2. The casino floorperson had Mr. Smith sign for the $500 marker and then started his rating slip. He began by entering the appropriate date and then entered Mr. Smith's name, the level of his casino credit, and whether the player was on a junket or is a regular, invited guest. The floorperson also recorded the table number on which Mr. Smith was playing.

At this point, the floorperson recorded the amount of the casino marker Mr. Smith had taken. If he lost this money and requested another marker, the floorperson would only have to enter the amount of the new marker on the line below the first marker drawn. The floorperson would not need to start another complete rating slip. However, some casinos have the policy that requires a floorperson to complete a rating slip for every marker taken at the tables, an unnecessary time-consuming and duplicated effort. It takes away from the time the casino floorpersons need to watch and protect your games.

The floorperson then recorded the time of day Mr. Smith began playing, and the amount of his first wager. As Mr. Smith played, the floorperson recorded the amount of his average bet. When he stopped playing, the floorperson recorded the total length of time he played, how much money he won or lost, and any appropriate remarks to help evaluate the player's value to the casino.

Master Action Record

When the floorperson completes the rating slips on each customer's play, they give the cards to a Casino Pit Clerk who then gives all of the completed rating slips over a specified period of time (e.g. every 24 hours or at the end of each shift), to a person who compiles the information from each rating slip onto the player's Master Action Record.

In today's world, all of this information is computerized. The key factors are automatically computed and a total analysis of the player's action is given to the appropriate casino personnel on an alphabetized printout every 24 hours. Printouts are available any time they are needed. In our sample case, we will use a manual system, but the results will be the same.

The Master Action Record lists the players' names and the amount of their casino credit and/or front money on the top of the page. The information is then taken from each pit-rating slip and entered into the Master Record. At the end of each day, all of the players' casino action is totaled.

Figure 4.2 Master Action Record

Smith John			$ 5000	
Name: Last, First			**Credit Line**	
DATE	**ISSUES**	**AVE. BET**	**TIME**	**WIN/LOSS**
15-Dec	500	60	2-1/4	-200
15-Dec	500	55	1-3/4	-300
15-Dec	500	50	2-1/2	+275
TOTAL	**1500**	**55**	**6-1/2**	**-225**
16-Dec	500	65	1-1/4	-500
16-Dec	1000	75	3	-375
16-Dec	500	60	2-1/2	**+600**
TOTAL	**2000**	65	6-3/4	-275
17-Dec	500	**100**	2	**-500**
17-Dec	500	500	1-1/4	-300
17-Dec	1000	100	3	-1000
TOTAL	**2000**	**90**	**6-1/4**	**-1800**
TOTAL	**5500**	**75**	**19-1/2**	**-2300**
AIRFARE REQUESTED: $350 **APPROVED BY:** Nick Gullo			**AIRFARE APPROVED:** **$250**	

Airfare

One of the most expensive items for the casino to pay for is the customer's airfare. Therefore, close control is maintained over this area by using the information obtained through the rating slips and the Master Action Record. When the players request an airfare reimbursement, a copy of their airline ticket is attached to an Airfare Disbursement Form, and usually held in the Casino Cage until they are ready to leave the hotel. This gives Casino Management an opportunity to check the Master Action Record to determine if the player's casino action warrants paying all or part of the airfare.

The casino executive who approves the payment of airfare completes the Airfare Disbursement Form in the following manner:

1. Enter the player's name, city of origin, and the amount of credit line on the top of the form.
2. Attach a copy of the airline ticket to the form.
3. Enter the amount of the ticket in the total line.
4. Enter the amount of the airfare the casino will pay on the authorized line. This amount is usually 5% of the player's credit line or front money; however, this is a policy decision of each individual hotel/casino.
5. The casino executive then enters the casino action of the player on the Disbursement Form.
6. The executive then signs the form as the authority for the Casino Cage Cashier to pay the specified amount to the player.
7. The customer must sign the disbursement acknowledging receipt of the money.

This disbursement form and a copy of the ticket are forwarded to the Accounting Department so the proper records can be maintained. See Figure 4.3: Airfare Reimbursement Form below.

Figure 4.3 Airfare Reimbursement Form

Name: John Smith
City: New York
Credit: $5,000 FM --

Total: $350

A/F AUTH. $250

Date	12/15	12/16	12/17		Total
Action	1500	2000	2000		$5,500
Bet	55	65	90		$75
Time	6-1/2	6-3/4	6-1/4		19-1/2
Dec	-225	-275	-1800		-2300

Auth. By: Nick Gullo

Customer Complimentary Criteria

When casinos invite players to come to a hotel/casino, executives should tell them what they must do in the casino to receive complimentary airfare, room, food and beverage privileges before they start to play.

The easiest (and wisest) way to do this is to give each guest, at hotel check-in or in a pre-arrival correspondence, a Qualifying Letter that contains all of the pertinent information necessary to qualify for complimentary privileges. It is a good idea to give them names of several hotel/casino executives to contact should they have any questions. A sample Qualifying Letter follows in figure 4.4.

Figure 4.4 Sample Qualifying Letter

WELCOME TO NICK'S HOTEL
To make your stay as enjoyable as possible, we wish to point out a few guidelines for you. You are a casino guest, and as such, are expected to gamble to qualify for complimentary privileges.

Credit at the tables will be issued in MINIMUM amounts of $500. Players leaving the tables with chips are expected to redeem their markers. The Casino Management is the sole and final judge of all ratings and qualifications.

1. The following requirements are necessary to qualify as a Casino Guest:

CREDIT LINE	B.J.	CRAPS	BACCARAT	TIME PER DAY
$5,000.	$50	Spread $.50	$.50	4-5 hours
$7,500.	$75	Spread $.75	$.75	4-5 hours
$10,000.	$100	Spread $100.	$100	4-5 hours

2. Casino action equal to your credit line along with the above-mentioned betting and time requirements is necessary for you to qualify for complimentaries.

3. To insure that you will receive credit for all of your play, keep your VIP Card handy. It is imperative for you to present your VIP Card every time you take a marker or change tables. Should you play for cash or table checks, please give the floorperson your name, so you may be given credit for the time you spend at the table.

You are entitled to sign for food and beverage in all areas of the hotel for yourself and one guest. All incidental charges, i.e., bottled goods, liquor, telephone calls and tips which are incurred during your stay must be paid prior to departure.

All guests are required to settle their casino account by either check or cash prior to departure. Our casino personnel will be happy to assist you in making show reservations at other hotels, however, complimentary courtesies will be limited to our hotel.

We hope your stay at Nick's Hotel will be most enjoyable.

Nick Gullo
Nick Gullo
President

CHAPTER 5: JUNKETS

Chapter Outline

JUNKETS

If a single word conjures up strong images of how a casino does business, it is "junkets." Upon hearing the term, most people imagine freewheeling, planeloads of casino customers on all-expense paid flings. In fact, running junkets is one of the toughest, most competitive aspects of marketing for casinos, the junket representative, and even for the players, who are required to meet more standards with each passing year. It is also one of the most carefully regulated areas of the casino business. State gaming officials pay extremely close attention to the way in which casinos operate junkets and to the people who run them.

Becoming a junket representative appears to be a very inviting idea. However, most people planning to take the plunge into the junket business have very little understanding of how such an operation works, whether from the casino point of view, or in understanding the requirement to meet strict regulatory criteria.

While traditional definitions of a "junket" and "junket representative" pertain to groups of casino players, a good junket representative must also provide a continual flow of individual casino customers. In fact, in a typical hotel's junket program, about 70% of junket players should come to the casino with a group, and 30% of the players should come as individual send-ins. An individual send-in by a junket representative is also referred to as a "splinter."

An active junket program should produce about 2,400 room nights per month or 8% of the total rooms per month of a 1,000-room hotel. The average player stays in the hotel an average of 3.5 nights per visit; therefore, if your junket program uses 2,400 room nights, you will have approximately 700 junket players in your hotel/casino per month. A minimum credit line and/or casino handle (action or play) per junket customer is usually $5,000; therefore, a 700-player junket program should produce at least $3,500,000 in casino action per month. A $3.5 million program per month ($42 million per year) is very important to the bottom-line of any casino operation, especially a 1000-room property.

To bring 700 guests per month to your casino through a junket program, you must have about 20 good junket representatives working for you in different geographical areas of the world. A good junket representative must have the ability to bring in or send at least 30 to 50 players per month to your casino. The only way to achieve this is to know or continually encounter a large variety of people and known casino customers.

The best representatives are those who have worked as a junket representative's assistant or part-time agent. This gives the assistant a chance to gain experience in handling casino players and an opportunity to build a following of known casino players.

Another successful background is that of a travel agent because they have access to names of people who continually go to Las Vegas or other gaming centers through their agency, and they become personally acquainted with many travelers. It is an advantage to understand the travel business, particularly in terms of having the ability to reserve airline seats on a regular basis at a reduced rate. The travel agents/junket representatives have an advantage because they also earn a commission from the airline when they sell a seat.

Another good background is that of a restaurant or lounge owner because they have a continual flow of potential casino customers. A junket representative will mail out about 1,500 invitations to players to fill a 50-player junket. With this in mind, a successful representative must have a large reservoir of players to draw from to be successful.

REPRESENTATIVE CONTROLLING AGREEMENT

An important document to the junket representative and the casino is the Controlling Agreement because it defines the terms under which the junket representative and the hotel/casino will function. It must be specified in all areas of the relationship, especially the area about compensation for the representative, the manner and degree to which the representative will be involved in credit, and the length of the agreement. The following controlling agreement (Figure 5.1) is only a sample. The controlling agreement can be in any form and the length will vary, but it will cover all of the essential points about the junket representative's employment with the hotel/casino.

Figure 5.1 Representative Controlling Agreement

Date: January 1, 2000
To: Henry Stow, New Orleans
From: Nick Gullo, President
Subject: Employment Agreement
Nick's Hotel will pay you a commission for each qualified player based on the following criteria:

CREDIT LINE	COMMISSION
$ 1,000.	$ 25.
$ 2,500.	$ 50.
$ 5,000.	$100.
$ 7,500.	$150.
$10,000. and above	$200.

Nick's Hotel will reimburse you or the player for the actual cost of the player's airline ticket(s), or up to 5% of the player's credit line, whichever is the lesser amount. The player must have a credit line of at least $3,500 to be considered for airfare reimbursement.
A qualified player is one who meets the following criteria:
a) Plays to his credit line.
b) Minimum bets of $50.
c) Minimum playing time of 5 hours per day.
Nick's Hotel is the sole and final judge in determining if a customer is a "qualified player."
You are not required to collect or to guarantee casino markers.
You are not allowed to sign a contract in the name of, or on behalf of, Nick's Hotel, without the express written consent of the President or Casino Manager.
Either party may discontinue this agreement by furnishing a 30-day written notice of cancellation.

Henry Stow
Junket Representative

Nick Gullo
President

VARIOUS TYPES OF JUNKETS

Just as there are different types of tour groups and different types of conventions that fill hotel rooms, there are also different types of junkets. Before determining which types of junkets to solicit, consider the marketable assets of the property and its particular marketing needs and goals. In many cases, it will be possible to bring in two or three different types of junkets at the same time. You must be careful, however, not to bring in two conflicting types of junkets that differ greatly in financial position and level of play. Some customers from one group might feel uncomfortable with the members of the other.

There are four different classifications of business that you can generally expect to receive from a junket program. They are as follows:
- ▶ Regular Junkets
- ▶ Mini-Junkets
- ▶ Up and Backs
- ▶ Junket "Splinters" (individuals).

Regular Junkets

A regular junket is a group of eight or more players brought to your casino by a registered junket representative. This group (junket) will consist of players who have an appropriate credit line or front money to enable them to qualify for full room, food and beverage complimentary privileges, and to have at least some portion of their airfare returned to them. The normal qualifying criteria for a player on a regular junket is an average bet of $50 to $100 and playing time of four hours per day, or 10 hours for a normal three-day trip.

In most casinos, the credit or front money level necessary to qualify for room, food, beverage, and airfare is at least $10,000. However, some of the smaller casinos reduce the qualifying criteria in an attempt to attract more customers. This is an acceptable decision to make as long as they first study the aggregate cost of this business relative to the average earning potential of the players for the casino. It is not advisable for properties to spend so much to attract gambling business that they have to win an exceptionally high percentage of the players' money just to break even or earn a marginal return on their investment. Do not depend on luck. Prepare a Feasibility Analysis of all potential junket business before you make a decision to bring the group to your casino.

A regular junket will stay in your hotel at least three nights, and sometimes four nights. The most common pattern for a regular junket is to arrive on a Wednesday or Thursday afternoon and depart on a Sunday afternoon. The reason this pattern is the most popular, and therefore the easiest to sell to your representatives, is because the customers only miss a couple of days of work due to the weekend.

Most of your regular hotel and casino customers come to your property on the weekend. This results in a high hotel occupancy level, heavy casino action, and steady business in the restaurants and showrooms during this time. Therefore, it is advantageous to bring junkets into your hotel/casino in a Sunday-to-Wednesday pattern. It makes sense to bring business to a property at the most profitable time.

Another factor to consider when computing the cost of a junket is the "opportunity cost." If a guest occupies a room on a complimentary basis when you could have "sold" the room for $50, you now have a $50 per night opportunity cost.

A regular junket is almost always brought to your casino buy the junket representative who organized the group; therefore, you usually have the extra expense of the representative's airfare, room, food and beverage costs, along with an opportunity cost. If it is a large group, the junket representative will bring an assistant and you will usually have to pay the assistant's airfare, room, and food and beverage costs. The size of the group must clearly be stated before you allow the junket representative to accompany the group or bring an assistant. The junket representative should be allowed to accompany a group of eight or more players and may be allowed an assistant, contingent upon bringing in 25 or more players to the hotel/casino.

In summary, a regular junket is a group of eight or more players with a credit line of at least $10,000 each. They usually stay at the hotel for three or four nights and receive complimentary room, food, beverage, and airfare. The junket representative usually accompanies the group to the property.

MINI–JUNKETS

A mini-junket is a group of eight or more players brought to your hotel/casino for only one or two nights. They usually receive a limited amount of complimentary privileges. These players usually only put up $1,000 to $5,000 in front money or credit.

A mini-junket program is considered "expensive" because the ratio of earning potential per player compared to the cost per player is low. The reason is that the player puts up a reduced amount of front money, and usually only stays at the hotel for one night.

As previously discussed, the earning potential of a customer is determined by the amount of money (or credit) the player has, the amount of time the customer plays in the casino, and the amount of wager. With a mini-junket, two of the three factors that determine your earning potential are reduced.

However, there are several good points to consider regarding a mini-junket. Because you require smaller amounts of front money or credit, it is easier to attract players. However, the quantity is greater, but the quality is reduced. Because you increase the quantity of casino players to your property through a mini-junket program, you may be able to reduce the number of rooms you sell to lower-priced tour groups. This is a big advantage because it provides you with a method to increase the revenue per room night by replacing lower revenue tour groups with casino-oriented groups, even if they are less lucrative casino players.

Most of the mini-junkets are brought to a casino on a cash-only basis. This is easier to do because the customer is only required to bring $1,000, compared to a regular junket with a minimum credit line of $10,000. The normal qualifying requirement for a mini-junket player is an average bet of $25 and at least five hours of play per 24-hour period. Because the mini-junket players bring cash, these groups improve the cash flow of your operation. This naturally eliminates credit and any potential loss incurred from bad debts.

A mini-junket program provides a casino with a steady flow of customers they can cultivate into regular, more profitable players. When players arrive in the casino, you should require them to complete a credit application for future trips. This gives you an opportunity to investigate them financially and to build a broader player base. It also gives players an established credit line in a casino where they are acquainted with a few casino executives. If they are in town at another hotel, they may now visit you to play in your casino.

Most mini-junkets offer limited complimentary food and beverage privileges, therefore, these groups will quite often provide your property with additional food and beverage cash revenue. For example, some casinos often host mini-junkets that receive complimentary buffet meals, but many of the players prefer to eat in the coffee shop or even in the gourmet restaurant. Some casinos offer mini-junket groups one meal on a complimentary basis, and therefore, over a 24-hour period, generate additional cash revenue for the restaurants.

A mini-junket program that only spends one night at the hotel can provide the flexibility of bringing the groups in on low occupancy days such as a Monday or Tuesday because the players only have to miss one day of work. The group leaves its hometown at 5 p.m. or 6 p.m. and returns to its home at 5 p.m. or 6 p.m. the following day.

A large number of players on mini-junkets are beginning players and, therefore, are sometimes less skilled in the finer points of casino-style gambling. As a result, the casino win percentage from these players is a little higher than normal. One of the most important aspects of the mini-junket is that casinos bring in players who could ultimately become a good source of regular business for a smaller property that may have a difficult time competing with the larger, ultra-deluxe properties. It is easier for the junket representative to "work" a mini-junket than a regular junket, because of the short turn-round time span, the less stringent qualifying requirements, and because the players require less supervision by the junket representative.

In summary, the disadvantage of a mini-junket program is the high cost per player relative to the potential profit because of a shorter playing time, the lower average bet requirement, and less front money or credit. The advantages of a mini-junket program include more flexibility regarding days of the week, higher quantity players, potential for an excellent source of future business, replacement business for less lucrative tour groups, and additional food and beverage revenue in the restaurants and bars.

UP-AND-BACK JUNKETS

An up-and-back junket is a group of eight or more casino players who bring a small amount of front money, usually $500 or less, and in return receive limited complimentary food and beverage and a portion of their airfare expenses. They do not receive a hotel room because they only stay in the hotel/casino from 8 to 12 hours.

The ratio between the normal earning potential of up-and-back players and the cost of bringing them to the casino is very small. This is very expensive business. However, because of the modest front money requirements and because they only have to be away for one day, it is easy to attract players to participate with this type of junket. An up-and-back junket program provides a casino with quantity not quality.

The most important aspect of an up-and-back program is the flexibility it can provide in supplying your casino with a group of players when the hotel/casino needs them.

You usually make an arrangement with a junket representative to bring a group of players to your casino on a regular schedule such as every Sunday afternoon or every Monday night or during slow periods when you need additional players, even if they are not high-profit players.

Up-and-back junkets provide more than flexibility in scheduling the arrival of the players. These groups can supply cash flow because you should always bring them in on a cash-only basis. They also provide an opportunity to develop a relationship with the good players on each trip. When casino executives notice a player who could benefit the property, they should introduce themselves and extend an invitation to return to the casino again in the near future.

The casino usually grants an up-and-back player one complimentary meal. Because the players are at the hotel/casino for up to 12 hours, they normally increase your food and beverage revenue because they eat additional meals or snacks in the restaurants.

Up-and-back junket programs provide players for your casino who can attract other players to the games much like a "shill." They are expensive "shills," but players at a gaming table will attract other players to the game.

An accepted "norm" win percentage for a casino is 20% of the amount of money handled. Therefore, if you agree to pay more than 20% of the customer's money on deposit, you will not make a profit from the player. You must consider your operating costs when analyzing the amount of money you can afford to pay for a player. For an up-and-back junket, the normal financial arrangement with the junket representative is to pay a pre-arranged amount for every player who deposits a pre-determined amount of money in your casino cage. For example, you agree to pay the junket representative $100 for every player who deposits $500 in your casino cage. Because up-and-back players only deposit $500 or less, it is not practical to give them a cashier's receipt to draw markers from the games. The easiest and most expedient method to use is to simply give them casino chips for the amount of their deposit.

Casinos use several methods to guarantee casino action by these players. The easiest method is to give them non-negotiable gaming chips. These chips are a different color than regular casino chips and the player is not allowed to cash them in at the casino cashier's cage. They must play all of these chips at the gaming tables. When the player bets a non-negotiable chip and loses the bet, the dealer deposits it in the table drop box. If the player wins the bet, the dealer pays the player with a regular casino chip but does not take the non-negotiable chip until the player loses the bet. This system accomplishes two things: it enables you to keep a record of the amount of gaming action received from the group; and it forces the player to gamble at least the amount of the "buy-in."

If you use the non-negotiable chip method, however, you must be careful the players do not "manipulate conditions" at the tables in an attempt to swap these chips without risking the possibility of suffering a loss. Often, two players on a dice table bet the same amount on each bet, one player bets the "do pass" line and the other player bets the "don't pass" line. Also common is to have a higher-skilled player on a trip play the non-negotiable chips for the weaker player. At first, this seems acceptable because the chips are being played. But since an up-and-back group is a low profit group, casinos depend on players of all skill levels to gamble.

A second method, the one found to work the best, is to give each player a numbered button and then record the amount of the bets each player made in a timed interval. An example of this type of analysis is the following up-and-back Players Analysis (Figure 5.2).

Figure 5.2 Up & Back Player Analysis

AL BROWN – SAN DIEGO
GROUP
SUNDAY – 10/18/00
DATE

Player's Name	Player #	1:00pm	2:00	3:00	4:00	5:00	6:00	7:00	8:00
John Adams	1	$5	$10	$5	$0	$0	$25	$25	$25
Bill Brown	2	$2	$5	$0	$0	$5	$0	$10	$5
Al Calucci	3	$10	$25	$25	$50	$50	$0	$0	$0
Frank Domique	4	$5	$0	$0	$0	$2	$5	$0	$0
John Edwards	5	$25	$50	$25	$25	$0	$0	$50	$100
Ed Fresh	6	$10	$10	$5	$0	$0	$0	$10	$10
Pete Christy	7	$50	$100	$50	$100	$0	$0	$0	$25
Harry Klarich	8	$5	$5	$5	$5	$0	$0	$0	$5
Bill Wilson	9	$25	$25	$50	$50	$30	$25	$0	$0
Sam Zenoff	10	$0	$5	$5	$10	$0	$0	$0	$0

Junkets

If, in the course of the player's entire stay in your casino, you do not record any play for that person, you should refuse to pay the junket representative for that player. This causes the junket representative to ensure every customer plays the required amount in the casino. This system of evaluating the players also prevents the representative from engaging in unethical practices. In the past some representatives have deposited front money for friends who did not play. This provided a free trip for the friends while the representative collected a fee from the casino to pay for the trip.

In summary, an up-and-back junket program is expensive, but it does provide you with players at times when you need them and cannot get regular, higher level players. It supplies you with cash flow and an opportunity to develop the good players from each trip into regular customers, and it can also furnish additional food and beverage revenue.

Individuals

Good junket representatives do more for a property than just bring junket groups to the casino. The junket representative is a delegate of a hotel-casino in a particular community. A representative has an opportunity to refer people to the hotel who are coming to the area for recreation and/or business. Since they have contacts with the business community where they live, junket representatives are also in a position to learn of future conventions in their planning stages. They have an inside opportunity to direct business to the properties they represent.

Because they constantly work with travel agencies, the junket representatives develop a personal relationship with a continual source of tour and travel business. However, the most important source of business from junket representatives, other than junket groups, is the casino-oriented customer they can send to your property on a regular basis.

A customer sent to a casino on an individual basis is referred to as a *junket splinter*. Junket splinters should account for approximately 25% of a regular junket program in terms of the number of players and the amount of casino handle. If this segment of your junket program runs as much as 25% of the total, it is very important to the bottom-line and you must cultivate this business.

Junket representatives help players with all of the details regarding travel and checking into the hotel. They arrange for the group's transportation from the airport to the hotel. They also make the hotel registration easier by pre-registering the players. They make certain all of the players' particular needs are pre-arranged. They make sure players have reservations in the better restaurants within the hotel and arrange for outside activities for players, such as golf or tennis, or shows in other hotels. In general, the junket representative is there to provide the necessary helping hand to make the players feel comfortable and enjoy themselves with a minimum of problems.

If you expect to develop this segment of the junket market, you must have casino executives who can handle this important function for the junket representative and ultimately for your property. You must make the guests feel welcome by putting forth the effort to make their visit to your property as trouble-free as possible. If you do not properly handle your casino guests, two things can happen to this area of business. First, the junket representatives will stop sending players to you on an individual basis because they do not want to take the chance of having their players neglected. Moreover, the representatives will not want to take a chance of losing the future business of a good customer because of dissatisfaction with the hotel/casino with which the junket representative is affiliated. Secondly, a competitor may end up with your poorly- treated customers. All people have egos, especially casino customers who are spending (losing) their money and, as such, they want to feel important. Guests of a hotel/casino come to your property because they want to relax, have fun, enjoy themselves, and escape from the trivial details of their daily routine. If you do not make it possible for them to enjoy themselves, you will no longer continue to enjoy their business—your competitor will.

In summary, the individual junket splinter market is very important to your bottom-line because it can represent as much as 25% of your total junket program, but you must have casino executives and/or casino hosts who can properly service the needs and desires of the customers.

JUNKET EVALUATION PROCESS

Before junket representatives can bring a group of players to your casino, they must submit the names to your Casino Marketing Office (or whatever department or office works with the representatives) for approval, and to prepare a rooming list for the Room Reservations Department. The names are then entered onto the Junket Group Player Analysis in alphabetical order. If you have a large group-- 30 to 50 players-- alphabetizing the names will save a considerable amount of time. During the three or four days the junket is in house, you will refer to the various players' records quite often.

Before the group arrives, you will have them pre-registered, their rooms assigned, and their casino credit already checked and approved, but you should not enter the room number or the amount of casino credit until after they arrive and you make all last-minute changes. Use the room number as a double check that the guest did, in fact, come with the group and is checked into the proper hotel room. This provides a safeguard for you to make certain a room does not remain vacant due to a last-minute cancellation, or that the player does not accidentally receive a suite of rooms which the casino intended to give to another more lucrative player with a similar name.

After all the players in the group have checked into the hotel and their credit is cleared at the cage for the proper amount, the Master Player Record pages are made and put into the player activity files. The rating from every marker taken in the casino will be entered on these pages. Every time a player gambles at a table in the casino, the floorperson must fill out a rating slip. The rating slip is the detailed account of the customer's activities in the casino. In fact, the information taken from the rating slips will determine how valuable a customer is to the casino.

Individual Player Ratings

The rating slips are the most important records you have of the customer's activities; thus, you must make sure to have a record of all of the players' activities. It can be embarrassing to deny a player an extension of complimentary privileges because rating slips show only $2,500 in casino action but the player presents you with $5,000 in markers. You should check with the Casino Cage or the casino pit records on a daily basis to reconcile the amount of markers taken to the number of rating slips for each player.

Figure: 5.3 Rating Slip

Date <u>10/18</u> D S X G_____

Name <u>John Adams</u>_____
Credit Line <u>5,000</u> FM_____
Reg_____Junket <u>Chicago</u>___

Dice_____BJ_____Roul_____

1ST BET	INDIVIDUAL MARKERS TAKEN	
25	$500	
Average Bet		
50		

WON_____LOST _____400
TIME IN <u>1:15</u>_____TOT <u>1 3/4</u>
                    TIME
_____
REMARKS: initials: <u>N.G.</u>

Steady Player

Master Player Record

The casino then takes information from each rating slip and posts it to the Master Player Record. Make sure to enter all of the information from every rating slip, not only so the customers will receive credit for all of their casino action, but because, when all of the rating slips are posted, it develops a pattern of the players' activity. For example, during the course of a three-day stay, Mr. John Adams has taken nine markers at $500 each for a total action of $4,500. However, on each marker, or session at the table, he only plays an average of 15 minutes, and he wins or loses only between $50-$100. Therefore, his pattern of play is established. This customer is not in your casino to gamble, and your chances of earning anything from his casino activities are very slim. You can make a decision from his activities to pay the junket representative neither a commission nor airfare for this player.

The information contained in the previous Master Player Record gives details contained on the rating slips, and includes all of the pertinent information regarding the player. This single record has the player's name, the dates of his stay in the hotel, the city he is from, the name of the person who referred him to your casino, how the property handled him (complimentary room, food and beverage), the room he occupied, the amount of credit he has, and the airfare and commission to be paid to the junket representative if the player qualifies

Figure 5.4 Master Player Record

Adams, John			10/19 - 22		$ 5000	
Name: Last First			**Date**		**Credit Line**	
Chicago			RFB			
City			**Status**		**Front Money**	
Schwartz			910			
Source:			**RM#**			
DATE	**ISSUES**	**AVE. BET**	**TIME**	**WIN/LOSS**	**RFB**	**RATING**
10/18	500	50	1 3/4	-400	--	--
	500	75	2	-300		
	500	50	1 1/2	+200		
TOTAL	**1500**	**60**	**5**	**-500**	**$95**	
10/19	500	100	1/2	+600		
	1000	75	3	-1000		
	500	60	1 1/2	-400		
TOTAL	**2000**	**80**	**5**	**-800**	**$125**	
10/20	500	50	3/4	-100		
	500	25	1/2	-100		
TOTAL	**1000**	**35**	**1 1/4**	**-200**	**$110**	
10/21	500	25	1/2	+50		
	500	25	1/2	-75		
TOTAL	**1000**	**25**	**1**	**-25**	**$ 75**	
TOTAL	**5500**	**50**	**12 1/4**	**-1525**	**$405**	
AIRFARE REQUESTED: $400				**AIRFARE APPROVED: $400**		
COMMISSION: $100				**APPROVED BY:** *Nick Gullo*		

Mr. John Adam's pattern on the Master Player Record is fairly well-defined as to what kind of a player he is. The first day, Mr. Adams plays at the table for an hour or more each session, and bets an average of $60 per hand.

His win/loss record indicates that he is a legitimate player and willing to win or lose several hundred dollars per session. The second day's records again indicate the same pattern. In fact, it shows that at one point he lost a full $1,000 marker in one session. However, on the third day he changed his style of play. He reduced the amount of his average bet and played for a shorter period of time. When he lost $100, he stopped playing.

On the fourth day, he again reduced the amount of his bets and played for a shorter period. It is obvious now that Mr. Adams is only drawing markers in an attempt to qualify. In other words, he is not willing to risk any more than he lost in the first two days.

Group Player Analysis

Everyday the information is posted to the Group Player Analysis from the individual's records on the Master Player Record. The Group Player Analysis form contains all of the names of the players the junket representative brought on a particular junket.

The junket representative meets with the junket coordinator for the casino every day to examine the activities of all of the players. They review the play of each player and the amount of their restaurant, food and beverage (R.F.B.) charges from the previous day. If the players are not playing to the expected levels, the junket representative has an opportunity to speak to them before the casino removes them from the complimentary player list, and before the junket representative loses the airfare and commission payment for these players.

On the Group Player Analysis form that follows, the casino pays the junket representative 8% of the player's credit line, or front money, for the player's airfare, and 2% of the credit line, or front money, the player's commission. Mr. John Adams qualified as a $5,000 player, so they pay the representative $400 for airfare and $100 in commission. Thus, a total payment to the junket representative of 10% or $500 is made for Mr. John Adams.

Ms. Samantha Franks' play does not qualify her for complimentary airfare, but the junket coordinator for the casino felt Ms. Franks played enough to pay the junket representative 2% of the $2,500 in casino action, for a total $50 commission. At this point, the representative has the responsibility to tell Ms. Franks that her casino action did not qualify her for complimentary airfare and therefore, she would be required to pay the junket representative the cost of her airline ticket.

When the junket trip is completed, and all of the casino action and the expenses involved are recorded, the information is then taken from the Group Player Analysis and a request for payment is made to the Comptroller's Office.

Figure 5.5 Group Player Analysis

Name	Front Money Credit		1st Day	2nd Day	3rd Day	4th Day	5th Day	Total	Air-Fare	Comm
ADAMS, JOHN	5,000	ISSUES	1500	2000	1000	1000	-	5500	$400	$100
		AG/BET	60	80	35	25	-	50		
		RF&B	$95	$125	$110	$75	-	$405		
		TIME	5	5	1-1/4	1	-	12-1/4		
BROWN, AL	10,000 FM	ISSUES	2000	2500	1500	3000	-	9000	800	200
		AG/BET	75	60	90	75	-	75		
		RF&B	$105	$125	$95	$120	-	$445		
		TIME	4-1/4	5	3-1/2	4-3/4	-	17-1/2		
CLEMENT, EDWARD	10,000	ISSUES	1000	500	2000	1500	-	5000	400	100
		AG/BET	35	50	30	25	-	35		
		RF&B	$95	$110	$125	$100	-	$430		
		TIME	1-1/4	2-1/2	2	3	-	8-3/4		
DAVIS, BOB	5,000	ISSUES	1000	1000	500	1500	-	4000	400	100
		AG/BET	25	25	25	35	-	25+		
		RF&B	$75	$100	$95	$105	-	$375		
		TIME	3	5-1/2	2-1/2	6	-	17		
DANIELS, ED	25,000	ISSUES	3500	2500	3000	4500	-	13500	800	200
		AG/BET	75	100	100	100	-	90		
		RF&B	$130	$125	$160	$150	-	$565		
		TIME	4-1/2	3	5-1/2	6	-	18-3/4		
FRANKS, SAM	5,000 FM	ISSUES	500	1000	500	500	-	2500	NO	50
		AG/BET	15	25	10	10	-	15		
		RF&B	$95	$100	$125	$75	-	$395		
		TIME	3/4	1-1/2	1/2	1/2	-	3		
GALLOWAY, BEN		ISSUES								
		AG/BET		C X	L					
		RF&B								
		TIME						Total	$2800	$750

Disbursement Request

To assure that the junket representative gets paid, and to have a fully documented record of payment in the junket file, casinos must submit a completed **Request for Disbursement Form** to the Comptroller's office. A copy of the request for disbursement should also be kept in the file, with a copy of the check sent to the representative as payment. This form and the check provide proof of payment, reason for payment, and it completes records for an audit (See Figure 5.6).

Figure 5.6 Request for Disbursement-Airfare

VENDOR CODE 107	DATE:	
	CHECK NO:	
	AMOUNT: $3550	
NAME AND ADDRESS:	**DISTRIBUTION**	
Mr. Howard Schwartz	**ACCT. NO.**	**AMOUNT**
Chicago, Illinois	Airfare	2800
REASON FOR DISBURSEMENT:		
Junket of October 18-22, 2000	Commission	750
	TOTAL	$3550
REQUESTED BY: *Harry Klarish*		
APPROVED: *Nick Gullo*		

Casino Groups Statistics

After compiling all the information pertaining to the junket, a complete analysis of the revenue and expenses regarding the group is important to determine whether it produced a profit or loss.

Several different methods and/or forms are used to compile the statistics of a junket, and to ultimately determine its profitability or value. Be aware, however, that the only way to really determine if you made a profit from a junket is to know whether you actually won or lost from the players on the junket. Compiling the pertinent information of each junket is of far more value than to use a 20% win factor for all the junkets. This method does not actually show if the casino made a profit from the junket being analyzed, but it does provide the ability to compare the casino handle and cost factors for each junket on an equal basis. You can compare "apples to apples" by using the following Casino Groups Statistics Form (Figure 5.7). When the form is complete, it will give you a good idea whether you made a profit or not. The easiest way, however, to determine the profitability of your junket groups, is to monitor the net win in the casino and subtract the actual cost of your promotional efforts, including the junkets.

Figure 5.7 Casino Group Statistics

PLAYERS	ROOM NIGHTS		AIRFARE	BAG & LUG.	COMMISSION	OUTSIDE EXPENSE	R.F.B.
6	24		$2800	$100	$750	$3650	$2615

Casino Expense	Cost Per Player			Issues	Hold	Revenue		
	A/F	Comm.	R.F.B	39,500	7900	Casino	Hotel	Total
$6265	467	125	436			1635	2615	4250

Average Revenue Per Player	Average Room Revenue	Average Issues Per Player		Cost Ratios		
				Airfare	2,800	7.09%
$708	$177	$6583		Handle	39,500	
				R.F.B	2,615	
Harold, The Average Issues Per Player Are Too Low. You Must Bring A Better Quality Player To Justify These Levels Of Expense.				Handle	39,500	6.62%
				Commission	750	
NICK				Handle	39,500	1.90%
				Total	15.61%	

This junket example consists of only six players to make it easier to analyze. These six players were at the hotel for four nights, for a total of 24 room nights. Their airfare cost was $2,800. No airfare was paid for the junket representative because only six players came on the junket. Baggage and luggage cost was $100, the cost of the transportation for the players from the airport to the hotel, and back to the airport. It also covered the cost of their baggage handling to and from the airport and their baggage handling at the hotel.

These six players earned a total commission of $750 for the junket representative. The cost of the airfare, baggage handling and the junket commission amounted to $3,650. This total cost is referred to as the *outside expenses* because this money was paid to people outside of the hotel/casino, as opposed to the *inside costs*, such as the complimentary room, food and beverage expenses. The complimentary room, food and beverage cost of $2,615 is an expense to the casino, but it is revenue for the hotel and Food and Beverage Departments. The casino expense of $6,265 is comprised of the outside expenses and the R.F.B. (inside) expenses. These are the total expenses of the casino for this junket. Dividing the total expenses of each area by the number of players arrives at the cost-per-player expenses.

The box marked "issues" shows the number of markers the players drew in the casino on this junket. This figure represents the amount of gambling these six players did, and the total amount they gave the casino a chance to win. However, this would mean the casino held 100% of the casino handle from them, while the normal hold is only 20%.

In fact, the hold figure of $7,900 represents 20% of the handle of $39,500. Casinos always use 20% as the hold percentage to make a fair and constant comparison of all the junkets. Areas analyzed prior to the hold figure are actual expenses, but the numbers analyzed thereafter, pertaining to the revenue, are based on the 20% hold estimation. Once again, this form does not claim to offer proof of a profit or loss. It is only an analysis and comparison tool.

The revenue for the casino of $1,635 is the difference of the $7,900 hold figure and the $6,265 total casino expense. The hotel revenue of $2,615 is the same as the complimentary room, food and beverage figure. It is classified as hotel revenue because this is the price the casino paid to the hotel and the Food and Beverage Department for their players' expenses incurred at the hotel on this junket. It is actually a paper transfer of funds from the casino win revenue to hotel revenue.

The total revenue-- the difference between the casino win of $7,900 and the *outside expenses* of $3,650--equals $4,250. Another way to reach the total revenue is to add the casino revenue of $1,635 and the hotel revenue of $2,615.

The average revenue per player of $708 is computed by dividing the total revenue of $4,250 by the total number of players, which is six. The average room revenue of $177 is computed by dividing the total revenue of $4,250 by 24, the total number of room nights. The average room revenue category is important to analyze because it provides the key to how much revenue per room night the junket produced. You should compare this number to the amount of revenue the room could have produced by renting it for cash to someone else, such as a tourist or conventioneer. Executives should also include the amount of food and beverage revenue, and casino win they could have received from the cash customer. For example, if the room rented for $30 per night to a cash customer, you would have had to generate $147 per day in food, beverage and casino win to equal the amount you earned with that room by housing one of these six junket players.

The average issues per player of $6,583 is the average amount of play you received by each of the six players. It can be computed by dividing the $39,500 in total issues by the six players. This figure is indicative of the quality of player on the junket. An average play of $6,583 is a very low average for each player. A good "regular" junket player should produce an average of $10,000 in casino play on a four-night junket.

The cost ratios are an extra tool used to analyze the value of the junket. The airfare costs to the total handle on this junket equated to 7.09%. To be profitable, this ratio must be at the 5% level. The only way to accomplish an airfare-to-handle ratio of only 5% is to have good quality players whose casino action is higher than the level of their credit or front money lines. For example, a $5,000 credit line player who produces $10,000 in casino action is more valuable to your bottom-line than a $5,000 player who only plays $4,000 in casino action. This conclusion is based on the assumption that all of the facts and playing habits of the two players are equal.

The R.F.B.-to-casino handle of 6.62% also is too high. This ratio again must be closer to the 5% level. There are two possible conclusions to analyze here. Is the casino handle of $39,500 too low, or did some of the players abuse their complimentary privileges by "overspending" in the restaurants, bars and showrooms? If the Casino Marketing Office checks the R.F.B. charges of the players every day, this is an easy area to control. If they do not stay on top of this area daily, it can create major financial problems and can cause an otherwise profitable junket to become a loser for the casino.

The commission costs compared to the casino handle is 1.9%; this ratio is also too high. It should be at 1% or below. The total cost of 15.61% is too high. The total ratio must be at the 10% to 11% level for a casino group to produce a profit. It is obvious from analyzing this junket that when casinos invite players who produce only $6,583 in casino action and receive full complimentary airfare, room, food and beverage privileges, and when the casino incurs a commission obligation for the junket representative, the casino cannot produce a profit for your property.

At the conclusion of the analysis form, you should add comments regarding the profitability of the group for the junket representative. This is a valuable communication tool to keep your junket program on a profitable level because it makes the representatives aware of the value of their players to your property. Forward a copy of the Casino Group Statistics form to the junket representatives for their records. Next, place a copy in the particular junket file for future reference. Then, set aside a copy for later use in completing your Monthly Marketing Report.

Individual Evaluations

You must evaluate every player coming to your casino who expects and/or receives complimentary privileges, especially if a junket representative sends them in and expects to be paid a commission. When the reservation is taken from the junket representative for the player, a Master Player Record sheet is prepared to record the customer's casino action after arrival at the hotel/casino.

As mentioned before, every time the player takes a marker, the casino floorperson prepares a rating slip:

Figure 5.8 Player Rating Slip

Date 10/22	DX__S____G____

Name James Jones
Credit Line 5,000_____FM_____
Reg.__Schwartz_____Junket_____

—

Dice_____BJ_____Roul_____	
1ST BET	INDIVIDUAL MARKERS TAKEN

1ST BET	INDIVIDUAL MARKERS TAKEN	
50	500	
Average Bet		
50		

WON_____LOST_____-300

TIME IN 3:00___ TOT _____2
5:00   TIME

REMARKS: initials: N.G.

Each rating slip is entered onto the player's Master Player Record, and at the completion of their stay at the casino, the ratings are totaled, and a casino executive makes the decision whether or not to pay for the player's airfare. The junket coordinator also makes a decision concerning the commission for the junket representative.

Figure 5.9 Individual Source Record

Jones, James			10/22 - 25		$ 5000	
Name: Last First			**Date**		**Credit Line**	
New York			RFB			
City			**Status**		**Front Money**	
Schwartz			1001			
Source:			**RM#**			
DATE	**ISSUES**	**AVE. BET**	**TIME**	**WIN/LOSS**	**RFB**	**RATING**
10/22	500	50	2	-300	--	--
	1000	100	1-1/2	-600		
	500	75	1-3/4	-200		
TOTAL	**2000**	**75**	**5-1/2**	**-1100**	**$125**	
10/23	500	50	1-3/4	+250		
	500	50	2	-300		
	500	75	3/4	-150		
	500	75	1-1/4	-400		
TOTAL	**2000**	**60**	**5-3/4**	**-600**	**$155**	
10/24	1000	100	3	-1000		
	500	75	1-1/2	-500		
	500	100	2	+3000		
TOTAL	**2000**	**90**	**6-1/2**	**+1500**	**$120**	
10/25	500	75	2	+200	25	
TOTAL	**6500**	**75**	**19-1/2**	**EVEN**	**$420**	

AIRFARE REQUESTED: $405	AIRFARE APPROVED: $250
COMMISSION: $100	**APPROVED BY:** *Nick Gullo*

Source of Business Records

The Casino Marketing Office maintains a source of business records for each junket representative. Every player for whom the representative makes a reservation is entered onto the representative's record. This record is prepared on a month-to-month basis. By handling the record on a monthly basis, it is easier to evaluate a representative's activities, and easier to locate the activities of a particular player when needed. The activities of each player are totaled at the end of the month in the same manner that a junket is evaluated, thus, giving you a better idea of the levels of the players.

Figure 5.10 Source of Business Record--Individuals

NAME	DATE	ROOM NIGHTS	CREDIT LINE	A/F	COMM	EXP	RFB	CASINO COST	HANDLE	HOLD	CASINO REV.	HOTEL REV.	TOTAL REV.
James Jones	10/22-25	3	5000	250	100	350	420	770	6500	1300	530	420	950
Al Smith	10/25-28	3	10000	375	200	575	465	1040	13500	2700	1660	465	2125
Max Weil	10/25-28	3	5000	250	100	350	275	625	5500	1100	475	275	750
Total		9	20000	875	400	1275	1160	2435	25500	5100	2665	1160	3825

MONTHLY JUNKET REPRESENTATIVE ANALYSIS

The information from each junket analysis, the Casino Group Statistics, and the information for every individual the junket representative sent to the casino (Individual Source Record) are combined for monthly total and analysis of all the business received by each junket representative.

The same areas that are analyzed for the junkets and the individuals are again analyzed, but for the total amount of business received for the month. These records are then incorporated in the Monthly Marketing Report. The following Monthly Analysis (5.11), examines the monthly total production of three separate junket representatives on an individual basis and the total production of the entire junket program for the month, which includes groups and individuals.

Figure 5.11 Monthly Junket Representative's Analysis – October

GROUP	# Players	RM. NTS	AIR FARE	COMM	EXP	RFB	CAS. EXP.	Cost Per Player AIR FARE	COMM	RFB	Issues	Hold	Revenue CAS.	HOT.	Total	Ave Rev Per Plyr	Ave Rm. Rev	Ave. Iss. Per Plyr
Chicago Schwartz	9	33	3675	1250	4925	3775	8700	408	139	419	65000	13000	4300	3775	8075	897	245	7222
New York Kertz	15	45	7560	1800	9390	6750	16110	504	120	450	165000	33000	16890	6750	23640	1576	525	11000
Dudy Ravkind	23	81	4427	2100	6527	7705	14232	192	91	335	149000	29900	15668	7705	23373	1016	289	6478
Total	47	159	15662	5150	20812	18230	39042	333	110	388	379500	75900	36858	18230	55088	1172	346	8074

JUNKET CREDIT

The credit policies and procedures you established in your everyday operation must be adhered to when granting credit to players referred to you through junket representatives. It is acceptable to consider a recommendation for credit by a junket representative. A representative however, should not be allowed to approve and/or guarantee credit in a casino; only authorized executives of your hotel/casino should do this. Having clearly defined credit procedures used in granting credit and insisting these procedures are followed in detail is mandatory. Do not allow anyone, including your own executives, to overrule and/or waive any procedures and safeguards you have established regarding policies. In most places, gaming credit is a legally non-collectible debt. Winning uncollectible money is of no benefit, and it is an even bigger disaster—and much more costly—to extend credit that creates a negative cash flow.

Credit Applications

The following credit application is a standard form that provides you with enough information to make a decision about extending credit to a customer, and in collecting the credit.

Figure 5.12 (A) Sample Credit Application Form

A B	C D	E	F G	H I	J	K L M	N O P Q	R	S T U V W X Y Z	ACCT.#		
										DATE OF APPLICATION		
										SEND MAIL TO HOME BUS.		
NAME LAST FIRST MIDDLE										SIGNATURE OF APPLICANT		
RES.ADD. TEL. # ( )										DR. LIC#		
										STATE EXP DATE		
CITY STATE ZIP										DATE OF BIRTH		
COMPANY TYPE OF BUS. TITLE										HEIGHT WT		
BUS. ADD. TEL. # ( )										COLOR HAIR: EYES:		
CITY STATE ZIP										SOC. SEC#		
NAME OF NEAREST RELATIVE RELATION										CREDIT CARD INFORMATION		
ADD. CITY & STATE TEL.# ( )										TYPE	SERIAL #	EXPIRES
MAX. CREDIT REQUESTED (PER 14 DAY TRIP) $												
AUTHORIZED CREDIT AMOUNT	DATE	APPROVALS								FOR OFFICE USE ONLY		
$										COMMENTS		
$												
$												

			How Ck'd	Date	For Amt	Good For	Not Good	
BANK #1	PERS. BUS.							
BRANCH	ABA#							
CITY	STATE							
ACCT.#	TEL.# ( )							
BANK#2	PERS. BUS.							
BRANCH	ABA#							
CITY	STATE							
ACCT. #	Tel.# ( )							

Figure 5.12 B (Office) Sample Credit Application

FOR OFFICE USE ONLY								

CENTRAL CREDIT		LIMIT	DATE EST	BANK CHECK	HIGH ACTION	LAST ACTIVITY	
DATE CH'D	HOTEL					DATE	AMT.

CUSTOMER DEPOSITS				SPECIAL INSTRUCTIONS AND DISPOSITIONS
Date	Amount	Date	Amount	

CHECKS CASHED			LEDGER ACTIVITY						
DATE	OK	AMOUNT	DATE	OK	PIT	IOU	R.C.C.	CREDITS	BALANCE

CHAPTER 6: SPECIAL PROMOTIONS

Chapter Outline

Special Promotions Description

Special Promotion Pre-Evaluation
      Pro forma
      Checklist

Special Event Customer Criteria

Evaluating a Special Event

SPECIAL PROMOTIONS DESCRIPTION

As stated in Chapter 4, a casino special promotion is any event used to attract a casino customer to your property before, during, and/or after the event. There are an unlimited number of variations and combinations of special promotions to create or participate in, but to simplify this segment of the marketplace, most special promotions are classified into two categories:

►   In-house promotions (active); and
►   Outside promotions (inactive).

In-house promotions are events created for your casino customers and hosted by the staff from your property. An example of an in-house promotion is a golf tournament, a tennis tournament, or a New Year's party.

The invitees for this type of event come from your regular players and from the players of your junket representatives. However, if a property is co-promoting an event with a charitable organization, you also have the advantage of introducing your property to new players through the mailing list of the organization members. A word of caution must be made here. While you do have an opportunity to gain new customers through a participating charitable organization's mailing list, you cannot afford to offer everyone complimentary rooms, food and beverage, and pay the promotional costs of the event in the hope of receiving casino action from everyone. You must invite all customers, especially people who have never been to your casino before, on a "must qualify" basis. This means either you must protect yourself by charging an entry fee to participate in the event, or you must extend complimentary privileges to the participants based solely on the level of their casino action.

If you allow junket representatives to invite their players to a special promotion, it is important to clarify how much commission, if any, you will pay for each customer who qualifies in the casino according to the normal criteria previously established and stated in their controlling agreement. This is a very important point because there are times when the promotional costs are such that properties cannot afford to pay a commission for the players who participate in the event. If this is the case, tell junket representatives before they invite their players to the promotion.

An outside promotion is an event hosted at another location; however, you invite your players to stay at your hotel while participating in the event. A perfect example of an outside promotion was the Caesars Palace Grand Prix. Almost every hotel/casino in Las Vegas invited casino customers to join them for the races. To participate in an outside event, your casino has the additional expense of the tickets for the race, as well as the expenses of complimentary room, food, beverage, and airfare for qualified players.

Another example of an outside special promotion is the World Series, especially if you have a Las Vegas casino and the Los Angeles Dodgers are playing in the Series. To promote the World Series as a special event for your players, you must make arrangements for their transportation to and from Las Vegas to Los Angeles, their transportation to and from the airport to the ballpark, and you must purchase their tickets to the game. These expenses are in addition to the normal complimentary expenses of room, food, beverage, and airfare.

When you invite players to the World Series, you should invite players who can provide you with enough earning potential to overcome these additional expenses. You can invite players to events like the Grand Prix who have a $5,000 credit line in the casino, but for the World Series you must invite players with a minimum credit line of $10,000.

Another type of outside promotion involves an event held at another hotel. You invite your players to stay with you and attend the other property's event. During the time of the customer's stay, you should include some additional activities, such as a poolside barbecue or a dance in the ballroom. The main reason for these additional activities during a special event is to make your invitation more attractive to the customer.

A major prize fight is an event in which it may be necessary to offer additional activities to the customers in an attempt to make your invitations more attractive than your competitors'. A major fight is an event that creates so much interest that every casino in Las Vegas uses it as a special promotion and invited players to join them at the fight. Even a casino that does not sponsor the fight may have several parties at our hotel in addition to offering our customers fight tickets. This is where evaluating the marketability of your property is crucial. Every other hotel/casino in Las Vegas would be inviting players for the fight, and if you invited the same players, those customers would naturally choose the more luxurious property. You also want to attract some of the players who would be staying at our competitors' properties to at least stop by our casino while in Las Vegas.

To accomplish these two goals, you may decide to participate in the fight by purchasing tickets and hosting a large poolside barbecue. You now had a competitive edge by making our invitation attractive to the players' spouses who were not interested in the fight. This also provided you with a way to get our customers to stay at your casino rather than going to a competitor's property for a show or to have dinner. At the same time, it attracts players staying at your competitors' properties to come to your casino.

In summary, special events can be classified into the following categories:

- ▶ events you host on your property only;
- ▶ events hosted by a competitor, but which you take advantage of by inviting your players to stay with you while they attend the event;
- ▶ events not hosted by any hotel/casino, such as the Super Bowl or World Series; and
- ▶ events hosted by a competitive property, in which you invite your players to stay at your hotel, attend the event at the competitor's property, then return to your hotel/casino for several special related functions after the event.

How To Pre-Evaluate A Special Event

Many special promotions appear as feasible endeavors on the surface, but collapse in the middle of the promotion and at that point executives realize the expenses are adding up faster than the possible revenue. Quite often, the only option available in these situations is to try to minimize the financial loss from the event. The sad aspect of this type of disaster is that the special event was an opportunity to make money rather than cost money. Yet, not only did you lose money on the bottom-line, but you also moved backwards at a chance to make a large profit. Most of the time, a substantial loss occurs with a special promotion because of poor planning. You should never agree to host or even participate in a special event until you take the time to complete a detailed analysis of that event.

Pro Forma

The following Pro Forma is an example of a pre-event and post-event analysis for the Tyson-Holyfield fight. There are many methods to evaluate an event, but this one is an excellent example because of its simplicity, and because it provides enough information to enable you to make a decision about the feasibility of hosting an event. This Pro Forma does not consider expenses like allowance for bad debts, and the normal operating expenses of the casino. These additional expense areas must be subtracted from the net win figure. Pro Forma analysis forms can become very complicated and time-consuming for casinos. Therefore, you should strive to ensure your forms do not become so detailed and complex that you find it necessary to devote more time to the form than to the actual event. The following Pro Forma could be used as an analysis tool to pre-evaluate the Tyson-Holyfield fight as a possible special promotion.

Figure 6.1 SPECIAL EVENTS PRO FORMA (Estimate)

TYSON / HOLYFIELD FIGHT AT THE MGM
&
TEXAS BAR-B-Q

DATE: _____

CONTACT: CASINO MARKETING OFFICE

PROMOTION: CASINO PROMOTION FOR $5,000 MINIMUM CREDIT
OR FRONT MONEY AND ABOVE

	ESTIMATED	ACTUAL
NUMBER OF PLAYERS INVITED	1500	
NUMBER OF PLAYERS	150	
AVERAGE CREDIT LINE	$7,500	
CASINO HANDLE	$1,125,000	
PROJECTED REVENUE :	$225,000	
CASINO	N/A	
ENTRANCE FEES	N/A	

PROMOTIONAL EXPENSES:		
AIR FARE (150 @ $250)	$37,500	
R. F. B. (150 @ $250)	$37,500	
INVITATIONS	230	
TICKETS (150 @ $100)	$15,000	
MAILING (1500 @ .18)	270	
CASH PRIZES #1	N/A	
#2	N/A	
#3		

COCKTAIL PARTIES:		
#1		
#2		
#3		

1

		ESTIMATED	ACTUAL
	#5	_____	_____
ENTERTAINMENT			
Country Western Band			
	#1	$250	_____
	#2	$250	_____
	#3	_____	_____
EVENTS:			
Poolside Bar-B-Q	#1	$5,000	_____
Open Bar	#2	_____	_____
Poolside Steak	#3	$4,000	_____
Buffet, Open Bar			
TOTAL REVENUE		$225,000	_____
TOTAL EXPENSES		86,462	_____
PROFIT		$138,538	_____

NO ONE WILL RECEIVE COMMISSION DURING THIS PERIOD

Detailed Information -- Pro Forma

CONTACT:

The Casino Marketing Office handled this event. This allowed all other departments and executives to know who to contact for information about the event.

PROMOTION:

This area provides all concerned with a narrative description of the event. This event is being hosted by the casino and the minimum level player to be invited must have a $5,000 credit or front money line. This information is important for all executives to have before they start inviting players.

NUMBER OF PLAYERS INVITED:

This is the number of invitations the Casino Marketing Office plans to send out. They felt that with every hotel/casino in Las Vegas inviting players to the event, they could expect only about a 10% acceptance rate.

AVERAGE CREDIT LINE:

Casino Marketing executives felt the level of play from each player would average $7,500, especially since they were hoping to receive some action from players staying at other properties but attending our parties.

CASINO:

This figure is the result of an average play of $7,500 multiplied by 150 players.

2

PROJECTED REVENUE:

Here again, we use a 20% hold figure. There is no expected revenue except from casino win. If it were a golf tournament, we could expect revenue from an entrance fee.

PROMOTIONAL EXPENSES:

This is a combination of all the expenses we anticipate for this event.

AIRFARE:

This figure was attained by multiplying the number of players times the average airfare amount we have been averaging per casino player. (We have the average airfare per player because we analyze every invited player who comes to our casino and record this information on a monthly report).

R.F.B.

This figure was attained by multiplying the number of players by the average restaurant, food and beverage expense per player. This information was obtained by analyzing our expenses per player. Then we made an adjustment downward because we were having two poolside parties. The players would eat there and, as a result, their average food costs would be reduced.

INVITATIONS:

The printer gave us an estimated cost of $230 for the 1,500 invitations.

TICKETS:

We bought 150 tickets at $100 each. We bought extra tickets in the event some of our players needed an extra ticket for spouses or friends; however, this was going to be an exception to the rule.

We also knew we could sell extra tickets if we did not use them for our players.

MAILING:

1,500 invitations at 18 cents each.

CASH PRIZES:

Not applicable

COCKTAIL PARTIES:

Not applicable

LIMOUSINE SERVICE:

We used our own limousine and hotel van to pick up the players from the airport. The three buses were used to transport our players to and from the fight. This is important because you want to provide transportation for your players to return to your casino. You do not want them to stay at the host hotel/casino or to walk to a nearby casino.

OUTSIDE PERSONNEL:

Outside personnel is not applicable. This would be used, for instance, for a golf tournament when you have score keepers on the greens and/or a golf pro to set up the tournament.

DECORATIONS:

We rented the scenery and props. For this event we used a western setting for our Texas Barbecue. The estimated cost was $800.

EQUIPMENT RENTAL:

The only equipment we needed for this event was a dance floor. Quite often, we have to rent additional sound and lighting equipment.

PHOTOGRAPHY:

Photography is not mandatory. However, it adds a nice touch to an event to take pictures of the guests, and it is a good source of future advertising if you take the photo near your hotel logo. In an effort to reduce expenses we did not use a photographer for this event.

MISCELLANEOUS:

We needed additional tables and chairs. The Las Vegas Convention Center loaned them to us at no charge.

ENTERTAINMENT:

We used a country-western band for both parties. To arrive at this figure, we had our Entertainment Director furnish us with an estimate. Do not simply guess at this type of expense. These areas can be very expensive if you do not control them.

EVENTS:

We hosted two poolside barbecues. Make sure you review the menu with your Food and Beverage Manager and Chef to get an accurate cost estimate. This is another area where you can experience very heavy cost overruns.

PROFIT:

The estimated profit was derived by subtracting the expenses from the projected revenue. Note the added comment that there will not be any commissions paid to the junket representatives for their players during this particular promotion. At this point, it is now possible to make an educated decision on the feasibility of this promotion. Our decision was in the affirmation based on a possible profit of $138,538.

4

Taking the time to do a Pro Forma on every event gives you an opportunity to analyze each area, and therefore, the total expenses of the promotion. An example of a couple of areas that could have turned this promotion into a financial loss was the cost of photography and the cost of the food. The photography expenses for this promotion could have been very expensive because research showed the price-per-picture would have been $10, which proved cost prohibitive to include with the invitation. The menu was revised three times before we arrived at an acceptable assortment of food at a reasonable price.

If we had just moved ahead with these two areas of the promotion without taking the time to research and analyze, we would have discovered too late that our expenses were higher than anticipated and, therefore, the profit of the event was not worth the effort or the risk to the casino. When hosting a special promotion, it is vital to continually review every detail of the promotion. A checklist is an excellent tool to ensure quality attention to these necessary details.

Special Promotions Checklist

The following type of checklist could be useful to monitor all of the details connected to a special event such as the Tyson-Holyfield fight promotion. Every executive involved with the promotion receives a copy of the checklist; they bring it with them to all of the meetings concerning the promotion. This keeps everyone up-to-date on the details of the promotion in terms of what has been handled and what remains to be handled to ensure a successful event.

Figure 6.2 Special Promotions Checklist

INVITATIONS PRINTED	7/20, ordered by Pete Christy will receive by 8/1
INVITATIONS MAILED	8/10-all mailed-local 9/10
CONFIRMATION LETTERS	Not applicable
GIFTS	Not applicable
PRIZES	Not applicable
PHOTOGRAPHY	Not applicable
TICKETS	8/1-order 150 @ $100 through MGM promotion office
AIR TRANSPORTATION	handled by individual players
GROUND TRANSPORTATION	8/15-ordered through L.V. Connections
FUNCTIONS: 9/15 ROOM	Poolside-Chief Engineer to handle
DECORATIONS	Kern for props-ordered 8/15 by Pete Christy
FOOD	Food & Beverage Manager menu by 8/15– approved 9/1
FUNCTIONS: 9/16 ROOM	Poolside-after the fight
DECORATIONS	Kern
FOOD	Food & Beverage Manager, Approved 9/1
FUNCTIONS: ROOM	Not applicable
DECORATIONS	
FOOD	
TROPHIES	Not applicable
SIGNS	In-house by Purchasing Dept.
ENTERTAINMENT	Country Western Band, signed 9/1
PLAYER LIST TO CAGE	Judi/Rita/CMO, by 9/14
MEMO TO EXECUTIVES	Nick Gullo- - sent 8/15
MISCELLANEOUS	

BUDGET:
The Pro Forma was completed and approved by the General Manager on July 15, 2000. Begin your special promotion early enough to handle all of the duties necessary to create a successful promotion.
ROOM BLOCK:
It is important to block the rooms required early enough to allow the other sales departments to adjust their sales efforts to coincide with the available rooms.
Disaster strikes when executives realize one week before the event that no one requested a room block and, as a result, the hotel is now oversold.

All of the areas of concern on the promotion checklist are more or less self-explanatory. You need to continually review all the details of the promotion with all executives involved. Special promotions can be high profit events and they also offer you the biggest opportunity to build a following of good casino customers for your property because players like to be considered regular customers of a casino that continually offers extra incentives to them. However, if you do not properly evaluate the event and every expense area of the event prior to making a commitment to it, you put yourself in the position of possibly suffering heavy financial losses.

SPECIAL EVENT CUSTOMER CRITERIA

After you complete the Special Event Evaluation Form, you know how much revenue you must generate to overcome the expenses and make a profit. Once you know how much revenue you need, you can then make a decision about the level of casino play necessary from each player to make a profit from the event. For example, if you expect 100 casino players at an event, which has a cost factor of $125,000, and you require the players to have an average credit line of $5,000, you will come up short.

100 players
$5000 casino action per player
$500,000 total casino action
20% win factor
$100,000 net casino win

If you are faced with this situation, you have two choices:

▶ You must invite players who have an average credit line of at least $7,500; or

▶ Make a decision not to host the event because it cannot generate enough revenue to overcome the expenses.

Once you have reached the point where you know what level of player you need to make your promotion a success, where do you get the players? Your database is an excellent place to start. If the criterion for this event is a minimum credit line of $7,500, look for the players who have a credit line of at least this amount, have been to your property at least once, and have a clear account with you. If these customers' previous quality of play, length of play, and method of payment are acceptable, then put their names on the list of potential invitees.

Going through the database of your regular players also gives you an opportunity to renew contact with some of your players who you have not seen for some time. Even if they are not able to accept your invitation for this particular event, they at least know that you value them as customers.

The next best source of business is the customer following of your executives. All executives should be informed of the details of the promotion, and the level of customers needed to make the promotion a success. It is much more effective to have the casino executives submit the names and addresses of their players to the Casino Manager's office or the Marketing Office and have them send an "official" invitation to the player. If executives are allowed to invite their players without going through the proper channels, the Marketing Department will lose control of the quantity and quality of the players invited.

The next best source of customers is from your junket representatives. However, it is important to make sure the representatives know the player criteria for the event, and it is equally important to make sure the representatives know if they will receive a commission for the players they send to the promotion. The most effective way to ensure accurate communication with the junket representatives about to your promotion is to communicate with them in writing only. Casinos should require representatives to submit the names of the players to your Marketing Office. Do not allow them to invite their players on their own. If you do, you again run the risk of losing control of both the quantity and quality of the players coming to your promotion. You must submit the names to the Marketing Office so they can screen the players before they send out the invitations, and to ensure the players receive an official invitation that clearly states the expected playing criteria in the casino.

The next source of possible business could come from an organization that has some particular interest in the event. If you host an event in conjunction with a charity, the organization connected with this particular charity might want to send invitations to its members. This could give you an excellent opportunity to introduce your property to new players. Once again, the invitations should be sent to the players through your Marketing Office. When inviting new customers to your casino through an outside organization, be very careful to explain in detail that you only extend complimentary privileges to customers who play in the casino to a specified level. This is a very easily misunderstood area. If you do not make certain invitees understand this point, you will have non-casino players refuse to pay their hotel bills because they "claim" you invited them to the promotion as a guest of the casino and/or the charitable organization. This can cause a challenge particularly when the event is a golf tournament and the customer pays an "entry" fee. Be specific when explaining that the "entry" fee only covers the golf tournament and not the hotel, food and beverage expenses.

In summary, you must evaluate all special promotions before you make a decision to host the event. Once the decision is made to host it, you must control and analyze the revenue and expense areas. Special promotions can be very profitable if they are controlled, but they can be a financial disaster if you do not attend to every detail.

EVALUATING A SPECIAL EVENT

After the players arrive at your casino for the special event, evaluate their casino action on an individual basis. Because the players will expect to receive complimentary room, food, beverage and airfare, you should follow the same individual player evaluation process as you would for a junket. After transferring the information from the Individual Rating Slips to the Player Master Record, then to the Group Player Analysis, you are ready to prepare the Final Group Analysis Form and complete the actual figures on the Special Events Pro Forma.

The following Pro Forma now contains the actual figures regarding this event. The information is self-explanatory, but a few key facts will be discussed.

Figure 6.3 Special Events Pro Forma (Actual Costs After Event)

TYSON / HOLYFIELD FIGHT AT THE MGM
&
TEXAS BAR-B-Q

DATE

Contact: CASINO MARKETING OFFICE

Promotion: CASINO PROMOTION FOR $5,000 MINIMUM
CREDIT OR FRONT MONEY AND ABOVE

	ESTIMATED	ACTUAL
NUMBER OF PLAYERS INVITED	1500	1500
NUMBER OF PLAYERS	150	150
AVERAGE CREDIT LINE	$7500	$7250
CASINO HANDLE	$1,125,000	$1,087,500
PROJECTED REVENUE :		
CASINO	$225,000	$225,000
ENTRANCE FEES		

PROMOTIONAL EXPENSES:

		ESTIMATED	ACTUAL
AIR FARE (150 @ $250)		$37,500	$25,500
R. F. B. (150 @ $250)		$37,500	$26,000
INVITATIONS		230	230
TICKETS (150 @ $100)		$15,000	$15,000
MAILING (1500 @ .18)		$270	$270
CASH PRIZES	#1	N/A	N/A
	#2	N/A	N/A
	#3	———	———
	#4	———	———
Brunch, Sept. 15 & 16	#5	———	$1,000

1

		ESTIMATED	ACTUAL
COCKTAIL PARTIES:			
	#1		
	#2		
	#3		
LIMOUSINE SERVICE:			
In-house Limo & Van	#1	$500	$500
3 Buses @ $166. Each	#2		
	#3		
	#4		
OUTSIDE PERSONNEL:			
	#1		
	#2		
DECORATIONS:			
Blaine Kern	#1	$800	$1,000
Western Props	#2		
	#3		
EQUIPMENT RENTAL:		$162	$162
9/15 Dance Floor, United Rent all			
9/16, 2 days @$81. (Debbie-333-3333)			
UNIFORMS:			
PHOTOGRAPHY			
MISCELLANEOUS:			
Table & Chairs	#1	N/C	N/C
	#2		
	#3		
	#4		
	#5		

		ESTIMATED	ACTUAL
TROPHIES		_____	_____
GIFTS:			
	#1	_____	_____
	#2	_____	_____
	#3	_____	_____
	#4	_____	_____
	#5	_____	_____
PUBLICITY		N/A	N/A
ADVERTISING			
SIGNS:			
	#1	_____	_____
	#2	_____	_____
	#3	_____	_____
	#4	_____	_____
	#5	_____	_____
ENTERTAINMENT			
Country Western Band 9/15	#1	$250	$250
Country Western Band 9/16	#2	$250	$250
	#3	_____	_____
EVENTS:			
9/15 Poolside Bar-B-Q	#1	$5,000	$2,700
Open Bar			
9/16 Poolside Steak	#2	_____	_____
Buffet, Open Bar	#3	$4,000	$600
TOTAL REVENUE		$225,000	$217,500
TOTAL EXPENSES		86,462	78,362
PROFIT		$138,538	$139,138

NO ONE WILL RECEIVE COMMISSION DURING THIS PERIOD

3

Details --Actual Pro Forma

AVERAGE CREDIT LINE:

We received an average play-per-customer of $7,250. We were pleased with the average and it was close enough to our projection to make our original Pro Forma valid.

PROJECTED REVENUE:

We actually held 19.99% of the casino handle where we hoped to be at the conclusion of this event.

AIRFARE:

We contained these expenses by concentrating on players from California, Texas and Louisiana. These closer areas have a lower airfare than areas such as New York or Miami.

R. F. B.:

As we expected, the actual costs fell below our normal costs because we had two poolside parties, with food, for the players to attend.

BRUNCH:

Due to the large number of guests in the hotel, we opened our Gourmet Room for a special brunch for VIP casino guests.

POOLSIDE PARTY:

September 16 – we were pleasantly surprised to have more people attend the "after the fight party" than anticipated. The additional play in the casino offset the additional cost of the party.

PROFIT:

The bottom-line profit resulted in what we expected because we pre-analyzed the event and controlled our expenses through every step of the planning and implementation of this promotion.

This event is a good example of how important it is to pre-analyze an event. If we had not controlled our costs and not properly projected our revenue, we could have experienced a substantially lower bottom-line.

CASINO GROUP STATISTICS

As previously discussed, it is prudent to prepare a final analysis of every event, junket, or marketing program you host in your casino. The final tool used to analyze the value of this or any other special event is the Casino Group Statistics. Let's run through the various areas of this special event analysis using the following Casino Group Statistics of our Tyson--Holyfield fight special promotion.

Figure 6.4 Casino Groups Statistics

FIGHT PROMOTION--TYSON/HOLYFIELD SEPTEMBER 15 & 16, 2000						
PLAYERS	ROOM NIGHTS	AIRFARE	BAG & LUG	FIGHT TICKETS & OTHER EXPENSES	OUTSIDE EXPENSE	R.F.B
150	450	$25,500	------------	$17,662	$43,162	$35,700

CASINO EXPENSE	COST PER PLAYER			ISSUES	HOLD	REVENUE		
	A/F	OTHER EXP.	RFB			CASINO	HOTEL	TOTAL
$78,862	$170	$118	$238	$1,087.500	$217,500	$138,638	$35,700	$174,338

AVERAGE REVENUE PER PLAYER	AVERAGE ROOM REVENUE	AVERAGE ISSUES PER PLAYER
$1,162	$387	$7,250

COST RATIOS	
AIRFARE HANDLE	2.34
R.F.B. HANDLE	3.28
OTHER EXPENSES HANDLE	1.62
TOTAL	7.24%

Breakdown of Casino Groups Statistics for Special Promotion— Tyson/Holyfield Fight.

PLAYERS: In this example, we succeeded in attracting the number of players we expected.

ROOM NIGHTS: The 150 players used 450 room nights. This means each player stayed at the hotel an average of three nights. Remember, some of the players arrived before the fight and some of the players arrived the day of the fight and stayed for the weekend.

AIRFARE: We experienced an average airfare of $170 per player for a total expense of $25,500.

BAGGAGE: Baggage was handled by each player on an individual basis. Therefore, we did not incur any expenses in this area.

FIGHT TICKETS & OTHER EXPENSES: The total cost of the fight tickets and other expenses outside the property was $17,662. These expenses come to an average cost per player of $118.

OUTSIDE EXPENSES: This amount was spent outside of the property, and included a combination of airfare and other expenses.

R. F. B.: This figure represents the total amount the casino paid the hotel for complimentary rooms, food and beverage, including the poolside parties and brunch. These expenses averaged $238 per player.

COST PER PLAYER: This area represents the average cost per player for their respective expenses.

ISSUES: This is the actual amount of casino handle we experienced during the time of this fight promotion.

HOLD: The amount the casino won during the time of this promotion. In this example we used the 20% figure.

CASINO REVENUE: The amount the casino won, less the amount of the cost to host this event ($217,500 less the $78,862 in expenses).

HOTEL REVENUE: This is the amount the casino paid to the hotel for the complimentary rooms, beverage and parties for the casino customers invited to this special event.

TOTAL REVENUE: A combination of the revenue earned in the casino and hotel as a result of the players invited to this event.

AVERAGE REVENUE This is the total revenue divided by the total number of players at the

PER PLAYER: promotion ($174,338 divided by 150 players).

AVERAGE ROOM REVENUE: This is the total revenue divided by the total number of players. This is an important area, because it represents earnings per room night in the hotel. It is a barometer by which we measure the quality of the player staying in the hotel. It is also an important measurement by which to judge the success of the promotion. In this case, if we did not have the promotion, could we have earned $387 per night for each hotel room we rented? The answer is "No."

AIRFARE/HANDLE: The airfare cost, 2.34% is excellent. We try to keep this area below 5%. Our attempt to keep the airfare cost down by inviting most of our guests from California was successful.

R. F. B. HANDLE: It is also important to hold this area below the 5% level.

OTHER/ HANDLE: This area represents the promotional expenses regarding the casino handle. This expense area should be held at the 1 to 2% level.

TOTAL: The total cost, 7.34% is excellent. Anytime this ratio can be held below 10 percent, the promotion should be a financial success, provided the casino wins at the gaming tables.

Chapter 7: Invited Guests and Casino Rate

Chapter Outline
Invited Guest Definition
Evaluating a Casino Host
    Reservation Forms
    Player Records
    Monthly Analysis
Casino Rate Definition

Invited Guest Definition

Invited Guests are customers who come to your hotel/casino because they are asked to do so by a member of your staff and/or because they like the physical amenities of your property. This segment of your Casino Marketing Mix is important because this portion of your business is usually comprised of premium (high-level) players, and should account for 10% of your total occupancy level.

There are basically three ways to attract individual Invited Guests to your casino:

▶ Through the appeal of the physical amenities of your property;

▶ Through the friendship of the players with a member of your staff; and

▶ Through the invitation of a casino executive (Host) whose primary function is to attract players to your casino.

First, many customers will be attracted to your property, and eventually become regular customers, because they like the physical structure of your hotel/casino and/or the physical amenities you have to offer. As an example, you may have a high-rise building of 20 floors. Some customers will stay with you because they enjoy staying in a high building with a good view of the city or ocean or the surrounding countryside. Other players will stay in a hotel because they like the style of architecture or the "feeling" they have when they are in your casino.

Still others will stay at your hotel/casino because you have an excellent golf course or health spa. The Desert Inn Hotel and Country Club in Las Vegas attracts customers on a regular basis because they have one of the most appealing golf courses in the United States. Other hotels are very successful in building a regular clientele of players who enjoy variety. The Bellagio Hotel has several of the best restaurants in Nevada. Caesar's Palace offers a top-rated shopping mall in the United States. These extra amenities do not exist by accident. They are planned and built to attract customers to the property, especially the casino.

Second, however attractive your property, it still depends on its employees to make each customer feel comfortable enough to want to return. Therefore, people who staff your property are very important to the success of your Marketing Programs. If you have people within your operation who "run" customers out the door as fast as you can bring them in, the best marketing efforts are doomed to fail. The opposite of this is also true. A large number of Invited Guests will return to your property because they meet and become friendly with members of your staff. These friendships do not need to be formed with the top-level executives. Many customers return to a hotel because a bellman or a front desk clerk made them feel welcome or they may enjoy eating in your coffee shop because the waitresses are always pleasant. Everyone likes to be recognized and made to feel important. It is of tremendous benefit to the success of your marketing efforts to communicate to your staff, and especially your casino executives, the importance of treating the customers well and trying to convert a one-time customer into a regular customer.

The third and most important element in a successful Invited Guest Program is the Casino Host. His or her primary duty is to invite customers to the hotel and casino, and to service the customers who are already playing in the casino.

EVALUATING A CASINO HOST

The most successful Casino Hosts are those who have worked within the hotel and/or casino industry for many years. During this time, they have become friends with a large number of players and, as a result, are able to invite them to the casino in which they are employed. This is referred to as the Casino Host's "following." These are the players who come to a property because of the Casino Host and not because of the property itself and/or a specific special event. The larger the "following" Casino Hosts have, the more valuable they are to your casino, because they bring more players into your casino than you ordinarily would have had. A Casino Host is a full-time salesperson and the product they sell is your hotel and casino.

Every successful marketing corporation continually evaluates the results produced by its salespersons. We recommend you follow the examples of IBM, Xerox, or any other successful marketing operation. These corporations continually appraise the performances of their salespersons in terms of revenue produced in relation to expenses.

If you use Casino Hosts in your Casino Marketing efforts, you must use a system to evaluate their results. A simple way to assess the revenue produced by Casino Hosts is to analyze the activities, casino action and expenses of every customer they bring into the casino.

Every reservation the Casino Host makes should have a copy forwarded to the Casino Manager's office or the Casino Marketing Office. A simple four-part reservation form with a copy for the casino office can be used.

Figure 7.1 An Individual Casino Reservation

DELUXE SUITE ACCOMMODATIONS	BONFIGLIO
	REFERRAL

NAME____M/M SMITH, JOHN_____

ADDRESS_____DALLAS, TEXAS_____

ARR.	DEP.	# OF PERSONS	FM OR CREDIT	QUALIFY
10/16	10/20	2	————————	

SPECIAL SERVICE   Complimentaries

Fruit basket to the room upon arrival   A/F_____

ROOM RES.   RFB_____

Near an elevator   R.M. Only_____

                                         F&B_____

1) ROOM RES.   Casino Rate_____

2) CAGE

3) CASINO OFFICE   Rack Rate _____

4) PERSONAL COPY   Must Qualify_____

The casino forwards the reservation form to the Room Reservation Department workers so they can make the reservation for arrival and departure on the indicated dates, and for any special instructions about the room accommodations requested. They also forward a copy to the Casino Cage so they will have all the necessary and pertinent credit information available when Mr. & Mrs. Smith arrive in the casino on October 16. The third copy goes to the casino office, to be recorded on the Host's monthly player record, and the final copy is for the Host's personal file.

As previously discussed, the casino records the activities of the player on Rating Slips and the Master Player Record. The results of the customer's casino activities and the expenses incurred during their visits to your casino are recorded in the Source of Business form or, in this case, the Host's individual player records. It is necessary to only record the player's name; the dates of stay in the hotel; room nights; credit line; airfare paid; room, food, and beverage expenses; and the amount of casino action received from each player. You will add the other pertinent information when you prepare the monthly summary of the Host's sales results. The commission section is the Host's monthly salary.

Figure 7.2 Host's Individual Player Record

INDIVIDUALS														
Mike Bonfiglio—October														
NAME	DATE	RM NHTS	CREDIT LINE	A/F	C O M M	EXP	RFB	CASINO COST	HANDLE	HOLD	CAS. REV.	HOTEL REV.	TTL REV.	R
JOHN ADAMS	10/1-4	3	5000	250			300		6000					
AL BROWN	10/2-6	4	10000	352			465		10500					
CHARLES JONES	10/8-11	3	25000	750			455		22000					
RUDY FAURIES	10/16-20	4	10000	265			350		9500					
FRANK ROMAIR	10/16-20	4	5000	250			375		7500					
JOHN SMITH	10/16-20	4	15000	405			325		16000					
JOHN HARTMAN	10/20-23	3	5000	--			275		3500					
HENRY STOW	10/23-27	4	10000	256			410		11500					
GAROLD GUGGIE	10/27-31	4	10000	500			425		18000					
LARRY GEISENGER	10/28-31	Casino	Rate											
GARIN DOYLE	10/28-31	Rack	Rate											

Figure 7.3 Casino Groups Statistics

CASINO GROUP STATISTICS MIKE BONFIGLIO OCTOBER 2000						
PLAYERS	ROOM NIGHTS	AIRFARE	BAG & LUG	COMM.	OUTSIDE EXP.	R.F.B
9	33	$3,028	----------	$2,000	$5,028	$3,380

CASINO EXPENSE	COST PER PLAYER			ISSUES	HOLD	REVENUE		
	A/F	COMM.	RFB			CASINO	HOTEL	TOTAL
$8,048	$336	$222	$376	$104,500	$20,900	$12,492	$3,380	$15,872

AVERAGE REVENUE PER PLAYER	AVERAGE ROOM REVENUE	AVERAGE ISSUES PER PLAYER
$1,764	$481	$11,611

COST RATIOS	
AIRFARE HANDLE	2.90
R.F.B. HANDLE	3.23
OTHER EXPENSES HANDLE	1.91
TOTAL	8.04%

You should use the same criteria to evaluate the statistics of the Casino Host, as you would use for the junket program. A Casino Host's salary should fall below the 2% level when compared to the amount of casino business they bring into the casino. The airfare expenses and complimentary room, food and beverage should fall below the 5% level for each. You should also record the number of players the host brings into the hotel who pay either the full hotel rate (rack rate) or a discounted casino rate. You should then add a "comment" relative to the host's monthly and year-to-date analysis forms.

If you emphasize the importance of your individual casino Invited Guest Program in relation to your overall Marketing Plan, and to the bottom-line success of your property, by continually analyzing to improve the efforts and, consequently, results of your Casino Hosts, you will have a successful program. You will know in a timely manner where the strengths and weaknesses lie within your "sales force." The secret of success in all areas of Casino Marketing is effort and control.

Casino Rate--Definition

A casino rate is a special, discounted room rate, which normally runs about 25% to 35% of the established room rate. This discounted rate is a valuable marketing tool that executives must be able to use easily and in a prudent manner. You cannot afford to indiscriminately give away 25% to 35% of your expected room revenue; therefore, this expense area must also be reviewed and controlled. This marketing tool should only be given to executives who have the authority to also extend complimentary rooms. This will automatically limit the number of people who have the authority to discount rooms, and these executives typically have more experience on your management team.

The controls and procedures to evaluate the complimentary privileges executives extend are already established. All you need to do is include this area in the evaluation process by having a copy of the reservations they make at a casino rate forwarded to the casino office. At the end of each month when the Casino Manager or General Manager prepares the Complimentaries and Invited Guest Analysis, this area could also be reviewed.

Properties should grant a special casino rate to some guests such as customers who play in the casino, but not high enough to qualify for a full complimentary room or patrons who contribute to the operation of the property in some positive manner. A good example is a top travel agent or the executive of a company who is staying at your hotel to discuss the possibility of a future convention for his company.

This casino rate is often extended to non-casino-oriented customers, perhaps to a friend of one of your higher level, regular casino customers. In that case, you extend this room discount as a courtesy to the regular customer.

In summary, a casino rate is a valuable marketing tool that has its place in a marketing strategy, but because it represents a definite reduction in room revenue, you must establish guidelines and controls in its use.

CHAPTER 8: BUS PROGRAMS

Chapter Outline

ADVANTAGES OF A BUS PROGRAM

A bus program is designed to increase the play in your casino, especially the Slot Department, by bringing customers into the casino for several hours at a time without occupying your hotel rooms. This program is designed to appeal to large numbers of players (quantity) with the expectation of receiving mostly slot machine play from them. These players produce a marginal amount of profit per player (low quality). The biggest advantage of a bus program is the possibility of attracting these players during slow periods such as the mid-week afternoons or early morning hours.

Because these players do not stay in your hotel rooms, it gives you the opportunity to sell the rooms for cash revenue or to extend a complimentary room to a higher-level player. A good bus program has a positive effect on the casino's slot revenue. Besides slot revenue, experience has shown that these customers can also affect poker and keno revenue, especially if they have promotional incentives to play these games. They also favorably affect pit game revenues but not as much as the slots, poker, and keno areas.

Bus Programs And Approximate Costs

The customers benefit from a bus program because it gives them an opportunity to travel from their hometowns to the various casinos for a very small fee. In some cases, they even receive the benefit of a free trip. Casinos make this possible by subsidizing the cost of the bus by paying the tour operator and/or bus driver to bring the customers to their casinos. This makes it possible for the tour operator to offer a "free package" to the customer.

Quite often, bus customers are required to pay $10 to $15 for the ride to the casino, but when they arrive, the sponsoring casino reimburses them for the ride, and sometimes gives them additional money. It is more advantageous to give the money to the customer instead of the tour operator because you have a chance to win the money back from the customer in the casino. Once customers start playing in the casino, they are more likely to continue playing with their own bankroll.

You can design a bus program to conform to the needs of your property more easily than any other source of business. Because of the mode of transportation, and the number of available buses coming to the casino area (Reno, Las Vegas, and Atlantic City), it gives them the flexibility to more easily fit into your available time slots.

Table 8.1 lists some of the more common bus stops in the Las Vegas area and the approximate cost of each type of stop. There is no limit to the variation of the type of bus stops available, or the price.

In most cases, like all other aspects of the economy, the price is determined by the supply and demand factors of the marketplace. Also, like every other aspect of the casino market, the more attractive and in-demand your property is, the less you will have to pay for the business.

Table 8.1 Sample Bus Programs and Approximate Costs

Bus Stop	Approximate Cost	Comments
1 Hour-First Stop	$75 to $100 per hour	The price will vary depending on the time of arrival. First stop means customers come to your casino before they stop at any other casino. The customers have more money and they are more eager to play in the casino on a first stop.
2 hour-first stop	$75 to $100 per hour	The group stops at your casino first and, they stay for two hours. You have more time to earn from the customers.
3 hour-first stop	$200, plus the cost of the buffet	This stop gives the customers a free buffet and the tour operator approximately $65 per hour.
4 hour-first stop	$300, plus the cost of the buffet	This stop gives the customer a free buffet and the tour operator approximately $75 per hour. The buffet is valued at $1 per player.
5 hour-first stop	$12 per person $25 commission	Each customer receives $12 cash, and the driver or agent is paid $25 commission per bus.
8 hour-first stop	$12 per person $100 commission	Each customer receives $12 cash and the driver or agent is paid $100 commission per bus.
2 hour-breakfast stop	$50 commission	This stop is used to attract groups that are in town overnight.
2 hour-buffet stop	$50 commission	This stop is designed to bring groups in at lunch or dinnertime. The player receives a free buffet and the driver receives a $50 commission.
1 hour-chicken and champagne	$25 commission	This stop is designed to attract the group on their way back home. Each person receives a boxed chicken dinner and free champagne for the ride home. The driver receives a $25 commission.
2 hour-chicken, champagne and bar	$25 commission	This stop is designed to attract the group on their way home. The passengers receive the chicken, champagne, and also a bar setup for the bus. The driver receives a $25 commission.
4 hour-second stop—buffet	$150 commission	The player receives a free buffet. The tour operator receives a $150 commission. This is a "good afternoon" stop on the group's first day in town.
5 hour-second stop—buffet	$200 commission	The player receives a free buffet. The tour operator receives a $200 commission. This is a good stop to fill in your slow periods.

Problem Areas Of A Bus Program

Every marketing area has some common control problems inherent to the type of business and customers who are a part of that market. A bus program has more problem areas that can cause a "leakage" of revenue and profits than most other markets because a bus program brings more drivers, agents, and more customers to your property at one time than the other markets, and the clientele of a bus program usually seeks value more than other markets. The following problems are the most common areas to investigate in your bus program, but they are not the only areas that you need to monitor.

When four or five buses arrive at your casino at one time and each bus has an average of 40 passengers, it is a time of chaos. The passengers want to get off the bus and into the casino, restaurants, or other areas, and each driver wants his people taken care of. Sometimes you will have five buses waiting to unload and you know that within the next 30 minutes you will have another 5 to 10 buses arrive at your front door. This situation is confusing and causes everyone, including the people in your Bus Department, to handle the groups in the most expedient manner possible. Rather than wait for the Bus Department personnel to check each bus before it unloads the passengers, the driver will tell his people to unload, and then report how many passengers were on the bus and how long they will stay in the casino. The Bus Department accepts the driver's word for this information and completes the necessary paperwork for the driver and/or agent to receive commission for the group.

Because between the time drivers arrive at a casino and when the customers exit the bus can create such chaos, some dishonest drivers have seized the opportunity to defraud casinos. A problem occurs when one person claiming to be a driver of a bus that just unloaded 40 people is actually a passenger on the bus, wearing a driver's hat and jacket and asks for and receives a commission for a busload of passengers. This type of fraud usually requires collusion with the real driver.

Another possible method of deception is when a driver drops off customers at one casino, then drives the empty bus to another casino at its busy time and submits a claim for a group. If the Bus Department clerk asks questions, the driver simply replies that the passengers would not wait on the bus long enough for the casino to check them in.

Another problem similar to these two examples happens when the driver drops off half of the passengers at one casino and the other half at another casino. This strategy enables the driver to charge each casino the full price.

Some of the groups who come to a casino receive "cash" coupon books. If they stay at your casino for an eight-hour period, you give them coupons to redeem for cash every hour. This provides an incentive for the group to come to your casino, and it also provides a method to retain the players. If they do not redeem the coupon every hour, they lose the remaining cash coupons in their book. Some drivers or agents claim they have 40 passengers and receive 40 cashbooks when, in fact, they only have 30 passengers. They can work a deal with one of the slot change persons to redeem the extra 10 cashbooks. They then split the profit.

If the drivers realize that your Bus Department does not count the passengers before they unload, they can inflate their passenger count. If the bus package includes complimentary incentives from the casino, such as free champagne and chicken dinners, the casino will give them extras they are not entitled to receive.

All of the problems described above are controllable if you schedule the buses so they do not arrive at the same time. Do not allow the driver to unload a group until someone from your Bus Department or security verifies the bus by number and driver, and then counts the number of passengers on the bus. You must make it your policy to pay a commission only for an unloaded bus and then require proper verification of the number of passengers on the bus.

After assurance that you have received the proper number of passengers from each bus that checks into your casino, you must verify the time the group checks out. Drivers or tour agents can check a group in for a two-hour stop and, after an hour, load the group back on the bus and take it to another casino for another two-hour stop. This means you pay twice as much for the group as you should have paid and your earning potential is decreased considerably because the driver has reduced the playing time of the group by 50%.

Sometimes drivers tell the passengers the stop is for them to stretch their legs or use the facilities. Then they drop passengers of at the front door of the casino and drive around to the back door and reload them. This entire process takes approximately 15 minutes. This gives them time to check in the group with the Bus Department and collect a commission. Your earning potential from this group is about zero.

You can control the problem of short time stops or no time stops if you time stamp the authorization for commission for the time of check-in and write the time drivers can pick up the commission at the Casino Cage. Do not pay the drivers the commission early and do not pay the commission if they do not pick it up within 15 minutes after the time of the scheduled departure. The best way to solve the problem of early departures is to have a security guard authorize the loading of each bus at the proper time. Give the security guard a copy of the driver's Commission Authorization form, which has the bus number and the time of check in and check out for the group. When the bus is loaded, have the security guard counter-sign the driver's Authorization for Commission form and then allow the bus driver to collect the commission from the Casino Cage.

Receiving a bus group as the first stop before another casino is more advantageous because the customer is more inclined to play and still has money. (In theory, the customer has not had a chance to lose money in another casino). Because your casino's earning potential from a first stop bus is higher, you can afford to pay more for the group.

One problem with this plan is that the driver or agent tells two or three casinos they are each receiving the first stop, and then collects the premium price from each casino for the group. If you receive the third or even fourth stop and yet you pay the first stop price, you may not make a profit from this group. The way to solve this problem is to use a bus spotter whose duties require a check of the buses as they enter the vicinity of the casino and record the bus number and the time of arrival. The bus spotter should also check competitors' parking lots and record the bus numbers and the times they were at other casinos. The Bus Department and the Internal Auditing Department should check this against commission reports. If you paid a driver for a first stop and you spotted the bus in a competitor's parking lot prior to the time it arrived at your casino, do not allow the driver to return to your casino. Once the drivers and tour agents realize you check this problem area, you will not be the one to receive the group on the second or third stop. If the spotter asserts a specific bus arrived in town at another location at 11 a.m., and the driver comes to your casino at 2 p.m. and claims that it is the first stop, you know this is not true. Your casino can therefore refuse to accept the bus as a first stop.

Bringing buses to your property on the first and the last stop basis is advantageous. When you coordinate your bus groups this way, it gives your property the most favorable times for the groups to gamble in your casino, the first and last.

One way to ensure the driver will not bypass your casino on the way out of town is to provide an extra incentive. Giving the driver a cash commission, and chicken and champagne lunches for the passengers can accomplish this. You must make sure, however, the drivers who show up for this particular stop also gave you the first stop, because most of the profit from this arrangement is in the first stop. To protect your casino, give the driver a pre-numbered form they must present to the food and beverage clerk. If the driver does not have this signed, pre-numbered form, the clerk should not issue the chicken lunches to passengers.

A bus program is designed to bring mostly slot players to your casino. Because of the nature of this type of business, and because of the extremely low financial requirements to go to a casino on a bus tour, this segment of the marketplace attracts value-seeking customers. Oftentimes, these players, and higher level casino customers are not compatible. Mixing the two markets can result in the higher-level players leaving your casino before you earn a profit from their casino play. As a result, you pay a premium price for the higher level casino player and at the same time you pay for another type of player who creates a situation that limits the earning potential of the more lucrative player.

Another problem casinos encounter when they invite bus groups is when the group is scheduled to stay at your casino from one to eight hours. When the passengers get tired of playing in the casino, they do not have a hotel room to go to, and because the driver usually locks the bus, the only place his passengers have to rest is within your property. This causes a problem because you now have a large number of people sitting in your restaurant, lounge, swimming pool area, and any other place they can find a seat. The problem is that they are no longer spending money and they take the seats from other customers who could be generating revenues for your property. The solution to this problem is to require all customers to purchase a minimum amount of food and/or beverages if they want to sit in these areas.

These are some of the more common problems you may encounter if you market your property to a large bus program. You can control and diminish these challenges, however, and you can earn a profit from a bus program. All markets have some inherent problems. Casinos must closely regulate these areas to minimize any potential damage.

CONTROL FORMS FOR A BUS PROGRAM

Properties should make every department aware of the business the casino will have on a daily basis, especially if it represents a large influx of customers. If you bring clientele to your property, and your revenue producing areas are understaffed, it can result in insufficient revenue production from the business you "bought" for your property. Notifying all departments prior to the group's arrival is important so they may properly schedule their employees. This way, departments will not waste payroll dollars from over-staffing when casinos do not have extra business, and they will fully staff when the business arrives, to maximize revenues. The following Charter Bus Arrivals Memo is simple but provides enough information to the necessary departments for them to properly staff, control, service and analyze the business.

Figure 8.2 Charter Bus Arrivals Memo

DRIVER GROUP NAME	PEOPLE	BUSES	DATE AND TIME ARRIVAL	DATE AND TIME DEPARTURE	TYPE PROGRAM
TO: SEE DISTRIBUTION				DATE:	
FROM: CASINO MARKETING OFFICE					
The following is a list of buses now booked and expected to arrive on the dates and times listed below:					
	46	1	10/30 11 p.m.	10/31 1 am	2 hr 1st
	40	1	10/30 11 p.m.	10/31 1 am	2 hr 1st
	40	1	10/30 midnight	10/31 3 am	3 hr 1st
	90	2	10/30 9 p.m.	10/30 midnight	3 hr 1st
	90	2	10/30 midnight	10/31 3 am	3 hr 1st
	40	1	10/30 midnight	10/31 1 am	1 hr 1st
	40	1	10/30 midnight	10/31 2 am	2 hr 1st
	43	1	10/30 midnight	10/31 3 am	3 hr 1st
	40	1	10/30 midnight	10/31 3 am	2 hr 1st
	40	1	10/30 midnight	10/31 2 am	2 hr 1st
	40	1	10/30 midnight	10/31 3 am	3 hr 1st
	40	1	10/30 midnight	10/31 3 am	3 hr 1st
	40	1	10/31 1 am	10/31 4 am	3 hr 1st
	40	1	10/31 1 am	10/31 4 am	3 hr 1st
	40	1	10/31 1 am	10/31 4 am	3 hr 1st
	40	1	10/31 1 am	10/31 4 am	3 hr 1st
	40	1	10/31 4 am	10/31 7 am	3 hr 2nd
	40	1	10/21 4 am	10/31 7 am	3 hr 2nd
	45	1	10/31 11 am	10/31 5 p.m.	6 hr 1st
	40	1	10/31 noon	10/31 4 p.m.	4 hr 1st
	45	1	10/21 1 p.m.	10/31 5 p.m.	4 hr 1st
	80	2	10/31 1 p.m.	10/31 5 p.m.	4 hr 1st
	40	1	10/31 1 p.m.	10/31 4 p.m.	3 hr 1st
	40	1	10/31 1 p.m.	10/31 4 p.m.	3 hr 1st
	45	1	10/31 1 p.m.	10/31 4 p.m.	3 hr 1st
	40	1	10/31 2 p.m.	10/31 5 p.m.	3 hr 1st
	41	1	10/31 2 p.m.	10/31 6 p.m.	4 hr 1st
	47	1	10/31 2 p.m.	10/31 5 p.m.	3 hr 1st
	41	1	10/31 2 p.m.	10/31 6 p.m.	4 hr 1st
	40	1	10/21 3 p.m.	10/31 6 p.m.	3 hr 1st
	40	1	10/31 4 p.m.	10/31 8 p.m.	4 hr 2nd
DISTRIBUTION: General Manager, Casino Manager, Food & Beverage Manager, Security, Casino Cage, Hotel Manager.					

Commission Payments

The most important area to control in a bus program is the commission paid for the type of group received by the casino. The greatest problem regarding commission payments to the driver is that the commission is based on several factors, and the payment and amenities given to the group and drivers come from several different departments. The following Commission Authorization Form simplifies the complexity of this problem for the Internal Auditing Department in reconciling the payments made by the various departments. This Authorization Form also provides an excellent source of information for the Security Department to run a spot audit of the information supplied by the Bus Department personnel. This makes it more difficult to overpay a driver and/or agent who supplies false or exaggerated information.

Figure 8.3 Commission Authorization Form

DATE:		No 8901	
NAME:			
BUS CO:			
BUS #:	NO. PAX:		
TIME IN:	TIME OUT:		
PACKAGE:	TOKE:		
FREE ROOM: yes no	No. NIGHTS:		
ONE FREE MEAL: yes no			
CHICKEN OR BAR RETURN: yes no			
DATE:	TIME:	No:	
C/C:	BAR:	BOTH:	
AUTHORIZED BY:			
WHITE COPY: Toke Authorization: (Driver – Present To Cashier's Cage 10 Minutes Before Departure To Receive Toke)			
BLUE COPY: Room Authorization: (Driver – Present To Front Desk Clerk For Room)			
GREEN COPY: Meal Authorization: (Driver – Present To Coffee Shop Waitress When Ordering. Good For One Free Meal Of Driver's Choice. (Alcoholic Beverages Not Included)			
CANARY COPY: (Chicken And Champagne Or Bar Order Form – Last Stops – Bus Office Presents to Chef)			
PINK COPY: (Driver's Receipt: Chicken And Champagne Or Bar Orders. Bus Office Presents To Driver Upon Last Stop Arrival)			
GOLDENROD COPY: (File Copy: Retained By Bus Office)			

The Commission Authorization Form is pre-numbered so you can match it on a daily basis to the number of buses you received in the casino. This enables the Auditing Department to reconcile the records of all the departments that make payments either directly or indirectly to the drivers, agents, or passengers of the Bus Program.

DATE

The date must be entered on the form. This prevents the driver from returning at a later date to collect the commission or other payments and it enables the Auditing Department to reconcile all of the records.

NAME

The name of the bus driver or agent who collects the commission is entered here.

BUS COMPANY

The name of the bus company and/or tour company on this line is important as identification of the source of business and the bus itself.

BUS NUMBER

This is an important identification tool. All buses are numbered.

NO. PAX

Entering the number of passengers is important so you can reconcile the payments made to the driver and also the number of "cash" coupon books given to the passengers. Remember, these books have a direct, immediate cash value.

TIME IN

The time that the bus and its passengers are checked into the casino.

TIME OUT

The time the bus and its passengers are allowed to leave the property. This also is the time the driver is allowed to collect his commission.

PACKAGE

This indicates the type of group this particular bus represents (e.g.--1-hour--first stop). It provides a double check on the length of time the group should stay at the casino and the amount of commission to be paid.

TOKE

This is the commission the Bus Department pays the driver or agent for the group. The Casino Cage pays the commission to the party named at the top of this form. They pay the amount indicated on this line. Because of the importance of this information, it should be written in ink.

FREE ROOM

This line tells the room clerk how to bill the driver for his room. If it is on a complimentary basis, the room clerk keeps one copy of this form as the authorization for the complimentary room.

NO. NIGHTS

This information is a further authorization for extending a complimentary room to the bus driver.

ONE FREE MEAL

This area is the driver's authorization to receive a complimentary meal. A copy of this form is attached to the bill for his meal in the restaurant.

CHICKEN OR BAR RETURN

This is an important area because the driver does not receive the pink copy of this form until the bus returns for the last stop on a first-last stop combination. The driver cannot pick up chicken and champagne or bar supply without an authorized pink copy of this form.

DATE/TIME/NO

This information is forwarded to the kitchen so they can prepare the food for this particular bus on the date and time indicated.

AUTHORIZED BY

An authorized employee of your casino signs here. Competent executives must control this because they are authorizing the payment of cash funds.

The bottom section of the Commission Authorization Form is an explanation of the use of each of the six, color-coded copies. After each department completes its part in servicing the bus group, they forward their copy of the control form to the Auditing Department. The Auditing Department uses these forms to reconcile the expenses of every department from each bus.

Daily Cost Report

Properties must summarize the individual costs of each bus on a daily basis. The Daily Cost Report is one method available to analyze the daily expenses of all the buses brought to your property in the aggregate. It provides the cost analysis of each bus and the totals of each day's bus promotional costs. This report must include the types of groups brought to the casino and the number of passengers within this category. The Daily Cost Report must also have the amount of expenses incurred relative to each player. The sample Daily Report (Figure 8.3) shows the casino spent $1 per player on all the groups except the six-hour, first-stop customers. This $1 per player is the estimated cost for the buffet meals they received. The $12 per player cost on the six-hour stop is the cash incentive you gave each player.

The next category states the number of buses brought to your casino in each category and the amount of commission (toke or tip) paid to each bus driver. The next category tells you how much you paid the tour agent for the group(s) and the manner in which you paid it. This information is important because it provides additional data to the Auditing Department in reconciling the cash standing of the Casino Cage.

The next section gives the number of hours each bus remained on the property and the total number of hours bus players stayed in your casino. This is an important statistic because your revenue is earned by the amount of the bet wagered and the time of play each customer stays in all areas of your gaming establishment.

The Daily Cost Report's final category is additional information for the Accounting Department. These statistics enable you to analyze the cost trends of your bus program on a per-hour cost, per bus cost and a per customer cost. The information from this report also provides the statistics for your daily and month-to-date general analysis of your bus promotional activities.

Figure 8.4 Charter Bus Office- Daily Report

							AGENTS' COMM CASH CHECK		BUS HOURS	ACCOUNTING DEPT. USE ADDITIONAL COST FACTORS		
PACKAGES		TOTAL								PER BUS	PER HOUR	PER CUST
	# P/P PAX	P/P COST	= COST	# BUSES X	AMT TOKE=	TOTAL TOKES						
1 HR 1ST	71	$1	$71	2	$50	$100	$ --	$ --	2	$86	$86	$2.41
2 HR 1ST	95	$1	$95	2	$100	$200	$--	$ --	4	$148	$74	$3.11
3 HR 1ST		$	$		$	$	$	$		$	$	$
4 HR 1ST	365	$1	$365	9	$ --	$ --	$	$2700	36	$341	$85	$8.40
6 HR 1ST	89	$12	$1068	3	$25	$75	$--	$ --	18	$381	$64	$12.84
2 HR BREAKFAST	94	$1	$94	3	$50	$150	$--	$ --	6	$81	$41	$2.60
3 HR REAKFAST		$	$		$	$	$	$		$	$	$
3 HR BUFFET		$	$		$	$	$	$		$	$	$
1 HR C/C	82	$1	$82	2	$25	$50	$--	$ --	2	$66	$66	$1.61
1 HR BAR		$	$		$	$	$	$		$	$	$
2 HR C/C		$	$		$	$	$	$		$	$	$
TOTALS (BY CATEGORY)	1040	$ ---	$1775	21	$ --	$575	$ --	$2700	68	$240	$74	$486
TOTAL BUS COST: $5050				DATE: 11-7-00					PREPARED BY: Nick Gullo			

Daily and Month-To-Date Activities Report

Certain areas require analysis of a bus program to provide the necessary information to determine the value of the program. This specific statistical information becomes even more significant if you compile the information on a month-to-month spreadsheet. A month-to-month spreadsheet enables you to easily spot any unfavorable trends that may develop within your program.

The first area to analyze is the total number of buses you brought to your property on a monthly basis. If you see this number declining, you have an opportunity to explore the reasons for the decline immediately, not after you have lost a significant portion of your bus program to competitors.

Next, is the total number of customers you brought to your casino and the average number per bus. This reveals if you are experiencing "light" busloads. After all, your earning potential comes from the bus passengers, not from the bus itself. This area should be dissected item-by-item to ensure all expenses were necessary.

Your casino's cost-per-customer, and cost-per-bus are the next areas to examine. These figures provide the information necessary to analyze the cost trend of your program. If your financial return is not what you expected, one possibility is that the costs for the buses and the players might be too high. If that is the case, you must immediately determine the reasons for the increased costs. Since the bus program is designed primarily to increase your slot machine revenue, compare the net slot win to the total Bus Department expenses. This comparison gives you a net figure for your slot win (slot win – bus costs = net slot win), and enables you to prepare a ratio of the slot win compared to each $1 in bus costs.

Table 8.5 Daily and Month-To-Date Activities Report

	Today	Month to Date
Number of Buses	21	181
Number of Customers	1040	7126
Bus Hours	68	488
Bus Cost	$5,050	$39,407
Average Cost Per Bus	$240	$218
Average Cost Per Customer	$4.86	$5.53
Average Cost Per Hour	$74	82

Figure 8.6 Bus Department Monthly Analysis

AREA	JAN	FEB	MAR	APR	MAY	JUN	JUL	AUG
TOTAL BUSES	545	600	841	725	686	750		
TOTAL CUSTOMERS	20615	24,000	34,000	26,825	24,915	31500		
CUSTOMERS PER BUS	38	40	40	37	36	42		
TOTAL EXPENSES	$185,000	$186,000	$265,000	$218,624	$190,000	$228,375		
COST PER BUS	$339	$3.10	$315	$302	$277	$305		
COST PER CUSTOMER	$8.97	$7.75	$7.79	$8.15	$7.63	$7.25		
SLOT WIN	$500,000	$550,000	$685,000	$546,000	$520,000	$665,000		
NET SLOT WIN	$315,000	$364,000	$420,000	$327,376	$330,000	$436,625		
SLOT WIN	$2.70	$296	$2.58	$2.49	2.74	2.91		
BUS COST	$1.00	$1.00	$1.00	$1.00	$1.00	$1.00		

CHAPTER 9: MONTHLY CASINO MARKETING REPORT

Chapter Outline

Explanation of and sample report which consists of the following:

    Financial Indicators Graph

    Casino Occupancy Report

    Junket Report

    Special Events Report

    Invited Guests Report

    Casino Rate Summary

    Bus Department Report

Summary

MONTHLY CASINO MARKETING REPORT

Casinos must evaluate every aspect of their Marketing Program as well as "sell" the casino to potential customers. In previous chapters, we examined the various markets from which to attract customers, and we also examined the various methods to evaluate every event you host on an individual basis. These individual event evaluations are essential to a successful marketing operation, but of equal importance, is to review your Casino Marketing Program in its entirety on a monthly basis.

A Monthly Casino Marketing Report is a useful tool to use to evaluate your overall Marketing Program on a current and year-to-date basis. This monthly review also provides an opportunity to make certain that your program continues to conform to your Yearly Marketing Plan, in terms of attracting the desired market, and in terms of profitability. The following Monthly Casino Marketing Report is a sample report to evaluate your program. Almost any report format will suffice as an evaluation tool provided it covers every segment of the market you use in your Casino Marketing activities.

APRIL
CASINO MARKETING REPORT
PREPARED FOR: Mr. John Smith, General Manager
                                   Mr. Robert Brown, Casino Manager
BY: Nick Gullo, Director Of Casino Marketing

CASINO MARKETING REPORT
APRIL 2000
I. Financial Indicators Graph
   a) Hotel Occupancy
   b) Casino Handle per Occupied Room
II. Casino Occupancy Report
   a) Junkets
   b) Special Events
   c) Invited Guests
   d) Casino Rate
III. Junket Report
   a) Narrative Summary
   b) Monthly Junket Summary
   c) Individual Representatives' Statistics
   d) Year-to-date Junket Summary
   e) Individual Representatives' Year-to-date statistics
IV. Special Events
   a) Narrative Summary
   b) Monthly Summary Report
   c) Individual Event Statistics
V. Invited Guests
   a) Narrative Summary
   b) Monthly Summary
   c) Individual Casino Host Statistics
   d) Year-to-date Summary
   e) Year-to-date Individual Host Statistics
VI. Casino Rate Summary
VII. Bus Department
   a) Narrative Summary
   b) Statistical Summary
VIII. Casino Marketing Summary
   a) Narrative Summary
   b) Statistical Summary

Financial Indicators Graph

The following lined graph provides a visual comparative analysis of our total occupancy level and the amount of casino handle we received per occupied room night. This comparison gives an indication of the value of the patrons who occupied our rooms. If the casino handle per room decreases while the occupancy level increases, it indicates that our Marketing Mix consists of too many non-casino-oriented sales and/or tour groups. This chart enables us to graphically note these important indicators by the month of the report and note any unfavorable trends that may develop in the quality of our Marketing Mix.

Figure 9.1 Casino Marketing Report: Financial Indicators Graph

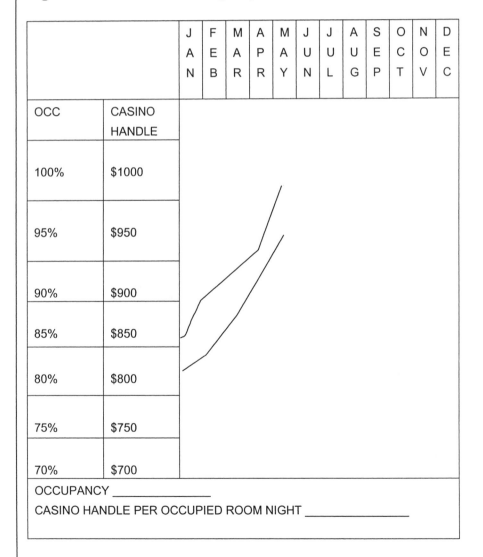

OCC	CASINO HANDLE	J A N	F E B	M A R	A P R	M A Y	J U N	J U L	A U G	S E P	O C T	N O V	D E C
100%	$1000												
95%	$950												
90%	$900												
85%	$850												
80%	$800												
75%	$750												
70%	$700												

OCCUPANCY _____

CASINO HANDLE PER OCCUPIED ROOM NIGHT _____

Figure 9.2 Casino Occupancy Report

	JAN	FEB	MAR	APR	MAY	JUN	JUL	AUG	SEP	OCT	NOV	DEC	TOTAL
JUNKETS	2127	3026	2756	2815									Room Night
	7.1%	10.2%	9.2%	9.4%									Percent
SPECIAL EVENTS	680	305	--	371									
	2.3%	1.0%	--	1.2%									
INVITED GUESTS	1800	2985	3600	1255									
	6.0%	9.9%	12.0%	4.2%									
CASINO RATE	425	296	370	310									
	1.4%	1.0%	1.2%	1.0%									
TOTAL	5034	7612	6726	4751									
	16.8%	25.4%	22.4%	15.8%									

Junket Report

In April the Junket Department surpassed its occupancy goal of 8% of total hotel occupancy by 1.4%. The junket players used 2,815 room nights, or 9.4% of the available room nights. Refer to Figure 9.3 that indicates the department brought 787 players to the casino this month and these players accounted for $6,881,800 in casino play, which averaged $8,744 per player. The average airfare per player was $365, a decrease from the $380 airfare per player in March. This improvement in airfare resulted from tighter controls when the casino rated the players. The average complimentary cost for room, food and beverage per player was $453. This figure shows an increase of $25 per player from March because we raised our prices in the showroom and the gourmet room. An in-depth analysis follows.

(This sample Monthly Casino Marketing Report only contains one page covering the individual junket statistics because it would be redundant to repeat several pages of individual statistics).

Figure 9.3 April Junket Summary

April Junket Summary Casino Group Statistics						
PLAYERS	ROOM NIGHTS	AIRFARE	BAG & LUG	COMM.	EXP.	R.F.B
787	2815	287,033	----------	54,860	341,893	356,120

CASINO EXPENSE	COST PER PLAYER			ISSUES	HOLD	REVENUE		
	A/F	COMM.	RFB			CASINO	HOTEL	TOTAL
698,013	365	70	453	6,881,800	1,376,360	678,347	346,120	1,034,467

AVERAGE REVENUE PER PLAYER	AVERAGE ROOM REVENUE	AVERAGE ISSUES PER PLAYER
1,314	367	8744

COST RATIOS	
AIRFARE HANDLE	4.17
R.F.B. HANDLE	5.17
OTHER EXPENSES HANDLE	.80
TOTAL	10.14%

Figure 9.4 Casino Group Statistics--Junket Representative Statistics-April

GROUP	REP #	PLAYERS	AIR/COMB EXP	RFB EXP	CASINO EXP	RFB	TOTAL EXP	COST PER PLAYER — AIR/COMB	COST PER PLAYER — RFB	COST PER PLAYER — CASINO	REVENUE — ISSUES	REVENUE — HOLD	REVENUE — CASINO	REVENUE — HOLD	REVENUE — TOTAL	AVE. REV PER REP	AVE REV PER PLAYER	AVE SI PER PLAYER
A	47	146	21,274	3,745	25,274	16,403	41,677	453	80	349	500,500	100,100	58,423	16,403	74,826	1,592	513	10,649
B	39	140	17,441	3,180	20,758	19,765	40,523	447	82	507	334,200	66,840	26,317	19,765	46,082	1,182	329	8,569
C	3	12	----	260	260	1,159	1,419	----	87	386	26,500	5,300	3,881	1,159	5,040	1,680	420	8,833
D	7	25	2,722	460	3,182	3,646	6,828	389	66	521	50,500	10,100	3,272	3,646	6,918	988	277	7,214
E	32	128	16,943	2,925	20,063	15,386	35,449	529	91	481	410,600	82,120	46,671	15,386	62,057	1,939	485	12,831
F	84	199	20,273	4,175	24,802	19,564	44,366	241	50	233	509,050	101,810	57,444	19,564	77,008	917	387	6,060
G	6	23	3,232	545	3,777	1,585	5,362	539	91	264	85,500	17,100	11,738	1,585	13,323	2,221	579	14,250
H	2	6	----	100	100	484	584	----	50	242	10,500	2,100	1,516	484	2,000	1,000	333	5,250
I	40	125	18,584	3,495	22,294	19,005	41,299	465	87	475	289,200	77,840	36,541	19,005	55,546	1,389	444	9,730
J	22	73	2,262	850	3,112	5,539	8,651	31	39	252	105,100	21,020	12,369	5,539	17,908	814	245	1,470
K	113	474	57,220	10,135	68,003	59,460	127,463	506	90	526	837,840	167,568	40,105	59,460	99,565	881	210	7,415
L	6	22	890	4,065	4,995	3,082	8,077	148	678	514	56,000	11,200	3,123	3,082	6,205	1,034	282	9,333
M	24	90	9,448	1,745	11,257	10,441	21,698	394	73	435	224,700	44,940	23,242	10,441	33,683	1,403	374	9,363

Figure 9.5 Casino Groups Statistics – Year to Date Junket Summary - April

PLAYERS	ROOM NIGHTS	AIRFARE	BAG & LUG	COMM.	TOTAL EXP.	R.F.B
\multicolumn{7}{c}{CASINO GROUP STATISTICS YEAR TO DATE JUNKET SUMMARY APRIL}						
2992	10,724	1,106,143	------------	217,145	1,323,288	1,300,384

CASINO EXPENSE	COST PER PLAYER			ISSUES	HOLD	REVENUE		
	A/F	Comm.	RFB			CASINO	HOTEL	TOTAL
2,623,672	370	73	435	27,518,610	5,503,722	2,880,050	1,300,384	4,180,434

AVERAGE REVENUE PER PLAYER	AVERAGE ROOM REVENUE	AVERAGE ISSUES PER PLAYER
1,397	390	9197

COST RATIOS	
AIRFARE HANDLE	4.02
R.F.B. HANDLE	4.73
OTHER EXPENSES HANDLE	.79
TOTAL	9.54%

Figure 9.6 Individual Representative Statistics–April

PLAYERS GROUP	#PLAYRS	RATING HRS	ACOMM	COMP	RFB	HOTEL	EXP	COST/PLAYER RATING	COST/PLAYER COMB	COST/PLAYER EXP	ISSUED	HOLD	CASINO HOTEL	HOTEL	TOTAL	AVE REV PER PLAYER	AVE REV PER HR	AVE ISSUE PER PLAYER
A	66	208	31834	5641	37892	25681	63573	482	85	389	683200	136640	73067	25681	98748	1496	475	10352
B	39	140	17441	3180	20758	19765	40523	447	82	507	334200	66840	26317	19765	46082	1182	329	8569
C	3	12	—	260	260	1159	1419	—	87	386	26500	5300	3881	1159	5040	1680	420	8833
D	9	31	4406	560	4966	4870	9836	490	62	541	67500	13500	3664	4870	8534	948	275	7500
E	41	164	19107	3570	22872	21059	43931	466	87	514	510800	102160	58229	21059	79288	1934	483	12459
F	123	354	34258	7050	41894	43643	85537	279	57	355	816350	163270	77733	43643	121376	987	343	6639
G	6	23	3232	545	3777	1585	5362	539	91	264	85500	17100	11738	1585	13323	2221	579	14250
H	3	11	175	175	175	923	1098	—	58	308	20500	4100	3002	923	3925	1308	357	6833
I	48	150	20099	4090	24404	22207	46611	419	85	463	450300	90060	43449	22207	65656	1368	438	9381
J	34	114	5322	1700	7022	10864	17886	154	50	320	193400	38680	20794	10864	31658	931	278	5688
K	1	4	—	—	—	859	859	—	—	859	68000	13600	12741	859	13600	13600	3400	68000
L	191	814	90396	16430	107822	115308	223130	473	86	604	1683340	336668	113538	115308	228846	1198	281	8813
M	29	115	5290	10065	15395	18219	33614	182	347	628	231700	46340	12726	18219	30945	1067	269	7990

Casino Special Events Report

In April we hosted two special events that brought 103 players to our casino for a total casino action of $1,502,850. The average casino action per player was $14,591. This figure illustrates the value of a special event because the average play per guest for these events was almost double the average casino action from our junket guests. The average revenue per player and the average room revenue from these promotions were exceptionally high, as well.

These statistical reports in summary follow. A detailed file of each report is maintained in the Casino Marketing Office should you care to study them in further detail.

Figure 9.7 Special Events Summary -April

SPECIAL EVENTS SUMMARY APRIL CASINO GROUP STATISTICS						
PLAYERS	ROOM NIGHTS	AIRFARE	BAG & LUG	COMM.	TOTAL EXP.	R.F.B
103	371	32,531	------------	12,958	45,489	30,463

CASINO EXPENSE	COST PER PLAYER			ISSUES	HOLD	REVENUE		
	A/F	Comm.	RFB			CASINO	HOTEL	TOTAL
75,952	316	126	269	1,502,850	300,570	224,618	30,463	255,081

AVERAGE REVENUE PER PLAYER	AVERAGE ROOM REVENUE	AVERAGE ISSUES PER PLAYER
2477	688	14,591

COST RATIOS	
AIRFARE HANDLE	1091
R.F.B. HANDLE	1.79
OTHER EXPENSES HANDLE	.76
TOTAL	4.46%

Spring Fishing Rodeo

In April we hosted our annual Spring Fishing Rodeo in San Diego. We invited 44 players to join six casino executives to come to Las Vegas for three days and then go to San Diego on a deep-sea fishing charter boat. Because of the limited number of players we could invite to this promotion, we had to be more selective than usual and therefore, we averaged $10,497 casino action per player. A further statistical analysis follows.

Figure 9.8 Spring Fishing Rodeo Casino Promotion

SPRING FISHING RODEO CASINO PROMOTION CASINO GROUP STATISTICS						
PLAYERS	ROOM NIGHTS	AIRFARE	BAG & LUG	BOAT	EXP.	R.F.B
44	176	10,731	----------	4,558	15,289	14,044

CASINO EXPENSE	COST PER PLAYER			ISSUES	HOLD	REVENUE		
	A/F	Comm.	RFB			CASINO	HOTEL	TOTAL
29,333				261,850	92,370			
	344	104	319			63,037	14,044	77,081

AVERAGE REVENUE PER PLAYER	AVERAGE ROOM REVENUE	AVERAGE ISSUES PER PLAYER
1,752	438	10,497

COST RATIOS	
AIRFARE HANDLE	2.32
R.F.B. HANDLE	3.04
OTHER EXPENSES HANDLE	.99
TOTAL	6.35%

Casino Fight Promotion

In April we were fortunate to have MGM sponsor a World Heavyweight Championship Fight. We only had 59 players at this promotion, but the revenue results were favorable. The casino averaged $21,034. This particular event was an exceptional success for our property. A complete statistical analysis follows.

Figure 9.9 Casino Groups Statistics - April - Casino Fight Promotion

CASINO FIGHT PROMOTION
APRIL
CASINO GROUP STATISTICS

PLAYERS	ROOM NIGHTS	AIRFARE	BAG & LUG	TICKETS	TOTAL EXP.	R.F.B
59	195	21,800	----------	8,400	30,200	16,419

CASINO EXPENSE	COST PER PLAYER			ISSUES	HOLD	REVENUE		
	A/F	Comm.	RFB			CASINO	HOTEL	TOTAL
46,619				1,241,000	248,200			
	369	142	278			201,581	16,419	218,000

AVERAGE REVENUE PER PLAYER	AVERAGE ROOM REVENUE	AVERAGE ISSUES PER PLAYER
3,695	1,118	21,034

COST RATIOS	
AIRFARE HANDLE	1.76
R.F.B. HANDLE	1.32
COMMISSION HANDLE	.68
TOTAL	3.76%

April Invited Guest Report

    In April we hosted only 319 players through our Casino Hosts. These players used 1,255 room nights or 4.2% of our total available rooms. We did not reach our goal of 10% of the available room nights because we also hosted two special events and many guests who would have come to our property through a Casino Host accepted the invitation to one of our special events. The average cost per player compared to the revenue generated was 8.39%. It is our goal to keep this ratio below the 10% level.

    At the present time, we have five Casino Hosts. It would be advantageous to increase the number of Hosts to eight. However, we must screen the applicants for these positions carefully because they will represent our casino to customers. We must make certain they have a large enough following of their own players to justify their salaries. An individual and a summary analysis follows:

Figure 9.10 Casino Groups Statistics - April -Invited Guest Summary

INVITED GUEST SUMMARY APRIL CASINO GROUP STATISTICS							
PLAYERS	ROOM NIGHTS	AIRFARE	BAG & LUG	COMM.		TOTAL EXP.	R.F.B
319	1255	103,665	-----------	15,000		118,665	117,620

CASINO EXPENSE	COST PER PLAYER			ISSUES	HOLD	REVENUE		
	A/F	Comm.	RFB			CASINO	HOTEL	TOTAL
236,285	325	47	369	2,185,200	563,040	326,755	117,620	444,375

AVERAGE REVENUE PER PLAYER	AVERAGE ROOM REVENUE	AVERAGE ISSUES PER PLAYER
1,393	354	8,825

COST RATIOS	
AIRFARE HANDLE	3.68
R.F.B. HANDLE	4.18
COMMISSION HANDLE	.53
TOTAL	8.39%

Figure 9.11 Casino Host Analysis -April

GROUP	# PLAYERS	ROOM NTS	AIRFARE	SAL.	EXP	RFB	CASINO EXP	COST PER PLAYER AIR FARE	COST PER PLAYER SALARY	COST PER PLAYER RFB	ISSUES	HOLD	REVENUE CASINO	REVENUE HOTEL	TOTAL	AVE REV PER PLAYER	AVE ROOM REV	AVE ISSUES PER PLAYER
JOHN ADAMS	42	147	15120	2000	17120	16170	33290	360	48	385	342300	68460	35170	16170	51340	1222	349	8150
AL BROWN	70	280	24150	4000	28150	28700	56850	345	57	410	546000	109200	52350	28700	81050	1158	289	7800
LOU CLARK	102	408	26520	4000	30520	33150	63670	260	39	325	938400	187680	124010	33150	157160	1541	385	9200
HARRY DAVIS	60	240	21000	3000	24000	22500	46500	350	50	375	606000	121200	74700	22500	97200	1620	405	10000
SAM EVANS	45	180	16875	2000	18875	17100	35975	375	44	380	382500	76500	40525	17100	57625	1281	320	8500
TOTAL	319	1255	103665	15000	118665	117620	236285	325	47	369	2815200	563040	326755	117620	444375	1393	354	8825

Figure 9.12 Year to Date Invited Guest Summary - April

CASINO GROUP STATISTICS YEAR TO DATE INVITED GUEST SUMMARY--APRIL						
PLAYERS	ROOM NIGHTS	AIRFARE	BAG & LUG	COMMISSION	TOTAL EXP.	R.F.B
2754	9,640	925,775	----	60,000	985,775	1,018,565

CASINO EXPENSE	COST PER PLAYER			ISSUES	HOLD	REVENUE		
2,004,340	A/F	Comm.	RFB	23,978,500	4,795,700	CASINO	HOTEL	TOTAL
	336	22	370			2,791,360	1,018,565	3,809,925

AVERAGE REVENUE PER PLAYER	AVERAGE ROOM REVENUE	AVERAGE ISSUES PER PLAYER
1,383	395	8,707

COST RATIOS	
AIRFARE HANDLE	3.86
R.F.B. HANDLE	4.25
COMMISSION HANDLE	.25
TOTAL	8.36%

Figure 9.13 Casino Host Analysis -April-Year to Date

GRP	# PLAY	ROOM NITES	AIR FARE	SALARY	EXP	RFB	CASINO EXP	COST PER PLAYER AIR FARE	COST PER PLAYER SAL	COST PER PLAYER RFB	ISSUES	HOLD	REVENUE CASINO	REVENUE HOTEL	TOTAL	AVE REV PER PLAYER	AVE ROOM REV	AVE ISSUES PER PLAYER
JOHN ADAMS	300	1050	108000	8000	116000	115500	231500	360	27	385	2460000	492000	260500	115500	376000	1253	368	8200
AL BROWN	643	2250	225050	16000	241050	257200	498250	350	25	400	5144000	1028800	530550	257200	787750	1225	350	8000
LOU CLARK	864	3025	237600	16000	253600	280800	534400	275	19	325	7516800	1503360	968960	280800	1249760	1446	413	8700
HARRY DAVIS	600	2100	225500	12000	237000	228000	465000	375	20	380	5700000	1140000	675000	228000	903000	1505	430	9500
SAM EVANS	347	1215	130125	8000	138125	137165	275190	375	23	395	3157700	631540	356350	137065	493415	1422	406	9100
TOTAL	2754	9640	925775	60000	985775	1018565	2004340	336	22	370	23978500	4795700	2791360	1018565	3809925	1383	395	8707

Casino Rate Summary

We extended 310 casino-rated room nights to 101 players, a 1.0% usage of available room nights. This puts us right at the monthly goal we established for this marketing area.

Bus Department Report

In April we brought 725 buses and 26,825 customers to our casino through the direct efforts of our Bus Department. However, the average busload was only 37 passengers and because we pay a commission on a per bus basis, the cost per player was higher than desired. This problem, and the disproportionate number of one-hour stops caused us to generate only $2.49 of slot win for every $1 we spent on our program. This is the lowest monthly win ratio we have experienced during the year. A statistical summary follows.

Table 9.14 April Bus Program Statistics

Total Buses	725
Total Customers	26,825
Customers Per Bus	37
Total Expenses	$218,624
Cost Per Bus	$302
Cost Per Customer	$8.15
Slot Win	$546,000
Net Slot Win	$327,376
Slot Win/Bus Cost	$2.49/$1

April Casino Marketing Summary

JUNKETS: The junket program has reached the player and occupancy levels that we have established as our goals. For the last three months this marketing area has exceeded these goals. The average casino action per player from the junket program was an exceptionally high average of $9,197. We also managed to keep our costs below the 10% level.

SPECIAL EVENTS: This month, we hosted two very successful special events. One event was our annual Spring Deep-Sea Fishing Rodeo and the other was a championship fight sponsored by the MGM. The two events brought 103 players to our casino and they used 371 room nights. The average casino action per player was an exceptionally high level of over $14,000. These events also enabled us to introduce our property to several new customers, one of the purposes of a special promotion.

INVITED GUESTS: Our Casino Hosts only attracted 319 players to our property this month. They used 1,255 room nights, which represents 4.2% of the available room nights. Our Hosts fell below their projected goals this month because we brought many of their customers to our casino through our special events. At the present time, our Invited Guest Program is not meeting its projected goals because we need several additional experienced Hosts to broaden our player base.

CASINO RATE: In April, we used 310 casino-rated room nights. This is exactly the number of rooms per month we projected for this area.

BUS PROGRAM: The bus program experienced too many buses with less than 40 passengers. As a result, the cost per customer was too high and the slot play relative to the expenses was too low. We also brought in too many one-hour stops. These stops did not give the players enough time to play.

SUMMARY: Our Casino Marketing Department is doing an excellent job of aggressively marketing our casino to all of the available markets. The main areas of concern are increasing the number of experienced Casino Hosts and reducing the costs per player of the bus program.

Table 9.15 April Casino Marketing Statistical Summary

Market Area	Room Nights	Percentage of Occupancy
Junkets	2815	9.4
Special Events	371	1.2
Invited Guests	1255	4.2
Casino Rate	310	1.0
Total	4751	15.8

Chapter 10: Establishing a Casino Marketing Department

Chapter Outline

Introduction

In previous chapters, we explored the various markets most properties use to attract customers to their hotel and casino. However, how do you apply this information pertaining to these various markets to your property in the form of a defined and practical Casino Marketing Plan? Let's assume the Board of Directors of a hotel/casino tells you they would like you to structure a "complete" Casino Marketing Department to plan and attract additional casino-oriented customers to their property.

Currently, they have a very profitable and well-managed property, but have concerns with the ever-increasing operating expenses, and the continuing increase in competition in the hotel/casino resort industry. They must begin to explore new markets to give them a broader customer base. Keep in mind as you approach this task that you will be responsible for recommending a method of attracting customers to their property. You will also be responsible for creating and developing a Casino Marketing Office to control and analyze the casino action and the expenses relating to bringing those customers to their property.

Your task now is to review their property to determine the various markets you could profitably attract to their hotel/casino, and then to present your ideas to them in the form of a written proposal. The following is a sample proposal that you could use to establish a Casino Marketing Office for a hotel/casino property.

CASINO MARKETING PROPOSAL
NICK'S HOTEL & CASINO
LAS VEGAS, NEVADA

PREPARED FOR:
BOARD OF DIRECTORS
MR. MICHAEL STEVENS
MR. NICKOLAS NELSON
MR. ANTHONY ROSS
MR. JAIME ALVAREZ
MR. ALBERT BROWN
MR. NICK GULLO

INDEX
1. Casino Marketing Philosophy
2. Modus Operandi
  a) Casino Marketing Office
  b) Regional Representations
  c) Promotional Exposure
  d) Special Events
  e) Casino Hosts
3. Player Analysis
  a) Qualifying letter
  b) Rating Slips
  c) Player Activity Report
  d) Monthly Player Record
  e) Monthly Source Record
4. Airfare
5. Credit
6. Job Descriptions
  a) Casino Marketing Manager
  b) Casino Marketing Secretary
Organizational Chart

Casino Marketing Philosophy

Nick's Hotel has one of the most beautiful facilities in Las Vegas, and features all of the physical amenities necessary to attract qualified casino customers to its casino. At the present time, Nick's Hotel invites customers through the efforts of the hotel/casino executives. However, this effort is a secondary function of the executives' job description and duties.

The gaming industry is one of the fastest growing industries in the world. There are now casinos opening throughout the United States, especially tribal casinos, and to compound this growth rate, most of the established ones are expanding. Logic dictates that the growth within our industry increases the competition for hotel and casino-oriented customers. The properties that do not make every effort to grow and to compete will meet a slow death at the hands of spiraling operating costs and increased competition. It is now necessary to actively pursue casino customers on a full-time basis to stay ahead of the competition. We recommend a Casino Marketing Department that can bring new emphasis on the pursuit of qualified casino customers on a professional, organized and controlled basis.

We should also pursue all levels of customers, from the $1000 player to the $10,000 player, and extend complimentary incentives to them based on their level of profitability. Our philosophy is that all players are welcome at Nick's Hotel and, as astute, professional managers; it is our obligation to control the costs in pursuit of those customers.

Modus Operandi

Casino Marketing Office

The CMO will establish for Nick's Hotel, a nucleus from which to organize a professional approach to a viable Casino Marketing Office. This office will be staffed with experienced marketing executives whose primary responsibility will be to attract casino-oriented customers to Nick's Hotel and Casino.

CMO Established Customers

The CMO executives will contact their personal casino customers through direct mail and telephone to extend an invitation for them to enjoy the hospitality of Nick's Hotel and Casino. They will also invite these players to visit Nick's Casino on their next visit to Las Vegas, even if they have already made arrangements to stay at a competitor's hotel.

Nicks Hotel and Casino Customers

The CMO is responsible for ensuring that established Nick's Hotel and Casino customers know they are valued. They must provide these customers with the names of executives to contact when they have a need in Las Vegas, either for themselves or for a friend. All people, particularly casino customers, want to know they are special and important. If casinos convey this message, customers will look forward to their next visit to Nick's Hotel and Casino.

Regional Representatives

All customers will be invited to Nick's Hotel on an individual basis, but we should also give consideration to allow a select few representatives to send us players on a commission basis. This enables us to broaden our customer base in a shorter period of time, and, because we will accept the players on an individual basis, we can maintain full control of our costs and pay a commission only after all casino markers are paid in full. The players sent to Nick's Casino through a regional representative on an individual basis will become acquainted with our executives in the CMO and the casino, thereby giving us an opportunity to bring them into our "family" of customers. We must to extend a 2% commission to the representative based on the customers' credit line or casino play, whichever is lower.

Examples:
1) A $5,000 player who fully qualifies in the casino would earn a $100 commission for the rep.
2) A $5,000 player who qualifies as a $3,000 player would earn a $60 commission for the rep.

Promotional Exposure

It may prove advantageous for us to host (on a very select basis) a couple of introductory cocktail parties in areas where we can attract a large number of players.

Example: New Orleans – Nick Gullo is very well known in New Orleans, and has been offered a complimentary party by a very influential friend, who happens to own a shopping center and banquet hall. He is willing to donate a party valued at about $10,000. All we need to do is furnish transportation, hotel arrangements, and the invitations.

Special Events

Until we have an opportunity to work with our casino pit personnel about servicing and rating our casino players, it would not be advantageous to invite a large number of players into the casino at one time. However, we should immediately begin inviting players to stay at Nick's Hotel and Casino to participate in a citywide or a competitor's special event. Some examples are MGM Tyson – Holyfield Fight and the Super Bowl.

Casino Hosts

Several qualified Casino Hosts in Las Vegas would invite customers to Nick's Hotel and Casino. This would give us an opportunity to quickly expand our player base; however, we must not entertain this marketing approach until we have had an opportunity to establish the CMO, and refined the procedures to a Marketing Program. When we do reach the point in time where this marketing approach may be feasible for our operation, we will establish the value of an in-house Host on a quota and commission basis.

PLAYER ANALYSIS

All players who come to Nick's Hotel and Casino are valuable to us as long as we evaluate their casino action prior to extending complimentary privileges. To do this we must tell the players in advance what we expect of them in our casino. This is called a Qualifying Letter. We must then monitor their casino action on a daily basis to properly extend complimentary privileges.

Figure 10. 1 Sample Qualifying Letter

WELCOME TO NICK'S HOTEL AND CASINO

To make your stay as enjoyable as possible, we wish to point out a few guidelines for you, our casino guest. As a casino guest, you are expected to gamble to qualify for complimentary privileges.

The following requirements are necessary to qualify for complimentary privileges:

CREDIT LINE	AVERAGE BET	TIME AT TABLE	COMP. PRIVILEGES
$1000.	$10.	2 hours per day	Casino rate room
$2500.	$25.	2 hours per day	Free room
$2500.	$25.	10 hours total time	R.F.B./no gourmet room
$3500.	$25.	10 hours total time	R.F.B./gourmet room one night
$5000.	$50.	10 hours total time	R.F.B./one airfare up to $250.
$7500.	$50.	10 hours total time	R.F.B./one airfare up to $375.
$10,000.	$50.	10 hours total time	R.F.B./two airfare up to $500.

Credit at the tables will be issued in maximum amounts of $500. Players leaving the tables with chips are expected to redeem their markers, and will be requested to do so.

To insure that you receive credit for all your play, keep your VIP card handy. It is imperative for you to present your VIP card every time you take a marker or change tables. Should you play for cash or table checks, please give the floorperson your name, so you may be given credit for the time you spend at the table. You are entitled to sign for food and beverage in all areas of the hotel for yourself and one guest only. All incidental charges, i.e., bottled goods, liquor, telephone calls and tips that are incurred during your stay must be paid prior to departure.

All guests are required to settle their casino accounts prior to departure.

Our casino personnel will be most happy to assist you in making show reservations at other hotels; however, complimentary courtesies will be limited to Nick's Hotel.

We hope your stay at Nick's Hotel and Casino will be most enjoyable.

Nick Gullo, President

Rating Slips

Figure10.2a Player Rating Slip (blank)

The most important information for our casino to know about a player is how much you can earn (win) from the player's action (gambling) in your casino.

Our earning potential from each player is determined by these factors:

- How much money the player has in cash, credit or combination of both;
- How much the player is willing to wager on each bet; and
- How long of a period of time the player is willing to play.

Every time a player goes to a gaming table, the casino floorperson (in the gaming pit) identifies the player and prepares a Rating Slip on his play. This is not a difficult task, but this plan takes you through each step in preparing a rating slip as the casino floorperson would have to do to complete the form.

In the example, the player, Mr. John Smith, on December 15, during the day shift, came to dice table #2 and requested a $500 marker. When

| Date_____ D____ S____ G_____ |
| Name_____ |
| Credit Line_____FM_____ |
| Reg_____Junket_____ |
| Dice_____BJ_____Roul_____ |

1st BET	INDIVIDUALMARKERS TAKEN	
Average Bet		

| WON_____ | LOST_____ |
| TIME IN_____ | TOT_____ TIME |

REMARKS: Initials:

he presented the proper identification to the casino floorperson, and his credit was checked, the player was given $500 in chips to start playing on table #2. The casino floorperson has Mr. Smith sign for the $500 marker and then starts his rating slip. He begins by entering the appropriate date and then enters Mr. Smith's name, the level of his casino credit, and whether the player is on a junket or is a regular, invited guest. The floorperson also records the table number on which Mr. Smith is playing, and the amount of the casino marker Mr. Smith has drawn.

Figure10.2b   Player Rating Slip (completed)

Date <u>12/15</u> D X S G <u>   </u>

Name <u>John Smith   </u>

Credit Line <u>5,000   </u>   FM<u>   </u>

Reg<u>   </u>Junket <u>New York </u>

Dice<u>   </u>BJ<u>   </u>Roul<u>   </u>

1ˢᵗ BET	INDIVIDUAL MARKERS TAKEN	
25	500	
Average Bet		
60		

WON<u>   </u>LOST <u>   </u> - 200

TIME IN <u>1:15   </u> TOT <u>   </u> 2 1/4
                  TIME

REMARKS: initials: N.G.

Bets.Propositions

If he should lose this money and request another marker, the floorperson only has to enter the amount of the new marker on the line below the first marker drawn. He would not have to start another complete rating slip. However, it is the policy of some casinos to complete a rating slip for every marker taken at the tables. This is a time consuming and duplicated effort by your floorperson, and is not necessary because it takes away from the time your casino's floorperson has to watch and protect your games.

The floorperson will then record the time of day Mr. Smith began playing and the amount of his first wager. As the floorperson watches Mr. Smith play, he will then record the amount of his average bet. When he stops playing, the floorperson will record the total length of time he played, how much he won or lost, and any remarks he thinks are appropriate to assess the player's value to the casino.

When floorpersons complete the rating slips on each customer's play, they give the cards to a Casino Pit Clerk, who, in turn, gives all of the completed rating slips over a specified period of time (e.g. – every 24 hours, or at the end of each shift), to a person who compiles the information from each rating slip onto the player's Master Action Record.

As our casino has a computer, the key factors are automatically computed and a total analysis of the player's action is given to the appropriate casino personnel. They print an alphabetized list of all the players in the casino every 24 hours. Printouts are available at any time casino personnel needs them.

In our sample case, we used a manual system, but the results are the same. The player's Master Action Record lists the player's name; the amount of their casino credit and/or front money is on the top of the page. The information is then taken from each casino pit rating-card and entered into the Master Record. At the end of each day, all of the player's casino action is totaled.

Each day the R.F.B. is checked and entered on the Player's Analysis Record. At the end of the player's visit to Nick's Casino, we record the amount of airfare we allowed the player, and then we total all of the pertinent information and enter it onto the monthly Individual Player Analysis, by source of business. The Individual Player Analysis is particularly important if we have more than one source of business. If we receive players from Casino Hosts, outside representatives, or the CMO, this record is the method we use to analyze the activities of every player sent to us by each source of business.

The Master Player Records are maintained in alphabetical order in a folder by month. These are permanent records that are kept in the CMO as a reference to a player's past activities and expenses. We always use 20% as our win percentage so we can make a consistent comparison of each player's activities in relation to the costs of bringing them to Nick's Hotel and Casino. This form is not used as a Profit and Loss Statement.

These records are maintained on a permanent basis and casino executives can use them at any time to verify a customer's action and the complimentaries the casino granted. These records provide an excellent auditing trail.

Figure 10.3 Individual Player Analysis

Smith, John			12/15 - 18		$ 5000	
Name: Last First			Date		Credit Line	
New York			RFB			
City			Status		Front Money	
CMO			901			
Source:			RM#			
DATE	ISSUES	AVE. BET	TIME	WIN/LOSS	RFB	
12/15	500	60	2-1/4	-200		
12/15	500	55	1-3/4	-300		
12/15	500	50	2-1/2	+275		
TOTAL	1500	55	6-1/2	-225	106	
12/16	500	65	1-1/4	-500		
12/16	1000	75	3	-375		
12/16	500	60	2-1/2	+600		
TOTAL	2000	65	6-3/4	-275	95	
12/17	500	100	2	-500		
12/17	00	75	-1/4	300		
12/17	1000	100	3	-1000	97	
TOTAL	2000	90	6-1/4	-1800		
TOTAL	5500	75	19 1/2	-2300	$298	
AIRFARE REQUESTED: $350				AIRFARE APPROVED: $250		
COMMISSION: N/A				APPROVED BY: Nick Gullo		

Figure 10.4 Individuals – Casino Marketing Office

				Schwartz--Chicago--October										
Name	Date	Room Nites	Credit Line	A/F	Comm	Exp	Rfb	Cas Cost	Handle	20% Hold	Cas Rev	Hotel Rev	Total Rev	R
John Smith	12/15-18	3	5000	250	None	250	298	548	5500	1100	552	298	850	N/A

CUSTOMER AIRFARE REIMBURSEMENT

As previously stated, one of the most expensive items for the casino to absorb for the customer is airfare. Therefore, executives maintain a close control over this area by using the information obtained through the rating slips and the Master Action Record. When the player requests an airfare reimbursement, a copy of the airline ticket is attached to an Airfare Reimbursement form, and usually held in the Casino Cage until the player is ready to leave the hotel. This gives Casino Management an opportunity to observe the casino action of the player, and check the player's Master Action Record to determine if the customer's casino action warrants paying all or part of the airfare. The casino executive who approves the payment of the customer's airfare completes the airfare reimbursement in the following manner. The casino executive:

- Enters the player's name, city of origin and the amount of credit line on the top of the form;
- Attaches a copy of the airline ticket to the form;
- Next enters the amount of the ticket in the total line;
- Enters the amount of the airfare the casino will pay on the authorized line;
- Then enters the casino action of the player on the reimbursement form;
- Signs the form as the authority for the Casino Cage Cashier to pay the specified amount to the player; and finally
- Must have the customer sign the reimbursement to acknowledge receipt of the money.

The reimbursement form and a copy of the ticket is then forwarded to the Accounting Department for proper record maintenance.

CASINO CREDIT

Executives should not change the credit policies of Nick's Hotel and Casino to accommodate the new emphasis on the solicitation of casino-oriented customers. However, due to the many new players coming to Nick's Casino who are known to executives in the CMO, the executives' recommendations on credit for these players should be considered. It will also be our policy to request each player to sign a statement that all markers will be settled prior to departure. This statement is attached to the back of the credit card on each trip. This will not guarantee payment by everyone prior to departure, but it helps to control the level of outstanding credit.

Figure 10.5 Airfare Reimbursement

Name: <u>John Smith</u>
City: <u>New York</u>
Credit: <u>$5,000</u> FM --

Total: <u>$350</u>

A/F AUTH. <u>$250</u>

Date	12/15	12/16	12/17		Total
Action	1500	2000	2000		$5,500
Bet	55	65	90		$75
Time	6-1/2	6-3/4	6-1/4		19-1/2
Dec	-225	-275	-1800		-2300

Auth. By: Nick Gullo

Figure 10.6 Sample Credit Statement

I hereby agree to settle all outstanding credit extended to me by Nick's Hotel and Casino prior to my departure.

———————————
Signature

———————
Date

Figure 10.7 Sample Job Description--Casino Marketing Manager

POSITION TITLE: CASINO MARKETING MANAGER

POSITION SUMMARY: Candidate is responsible for all of the marketing needs of the casino. It is the candidate's responsibility to develop and implement Marketing Programs to provide the property with a sufficient casino handle/revenue per room to make the property profitable.

REPORTS TO: PRESIDENT

POSITION ELEMENTS:

Job Complexity: Candidate must have a casino and marketing background to properly coordinate the casino needs with the hotel sales and room reservation's needs to insure a proper hotel mix. Candidate must assist the Casino Manager in all areas of marketing and evaluate programs. Candidate must be capable of dealing with the Junket Reps, the casino and hotel customer and the other department heads on a level that is conducive to achieving the desired cooperation. Candidate must have the ability to go into the casino gaming areas and relate to both the executives and the players. Candidate must be capable of assisting the President and the Comptroller in any areas that said assistance is requested. Candidate must be capable of writing and presenting major property marketing summaries. Candidate must be capable of communicating with top corporate executives to assist hotel sales. Candidate must possess the inventiveness and creativity to bring good casino promotions into the property. Candidate must have "contacts" throughout the U.S. and the gaming industry to benefit the property.

CONTACTS:

Works very closely with the President, Casino Manager, Hotel Sales Manager, Comptroller and Casino Hosts.

KNOWLEDGE REQUIREMENTS:

EDUCATION: Open — Requires the ability to intelligently communicate verbally and through written expression to accomplish the task assigned.

College degree is very helpful, as is a good business and marketing background.

EXPERIENCE: Knowledge of casino/hotel operations is essential. Candidate should have experience in casino games and management, as well as marketing.

Figure 10.8 Sample Job Description-- Marketing Secretary

POSITION TITLE: CASINO MARKETING SECRETARY

POSITION SUMMARY:

Must possess the ability to coordinate the details of a Casino Marketing Program with the various departments on the property. Candidate must be a well-organized person with the ability to handle the casino customers and the administrative responsibilities of the Casino Marketing Office. Candidate must be capable of exercising sound judgment during periods of crisis and extreme pressure.

REPORTS TO: CASINO MARKETING MANAGER

POSITION ELEMENTS:

CONTACTS: Works with the Hotel Manager, Auditing Office, and the Casino Marketing Manager.

KNOWLEDGE REQUIREMENTS:

EDUCATION:

Open--Requires the ability to handle the routine secretarial tasks of an office (shorthand not required) but must have the ability and temperament to handle the casino customers.

EXPERIENCE:

Must have experience in the casino/hotel field and secretarial experience.

Figure 10.9 Organizational Chart

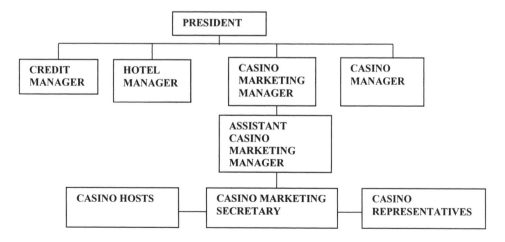

CHAPTER 11: SLOT MARKETING

Chapter Outline
Slot Marketing
    Slot Clubs

SLOT MARKETING

In today's casino world most of the day-to-day marketing emphasis is directed at attracting slot players into the casino. In some properties, all of the marketing efforts are directed at the slot-player market because it produces high volume in both customers and gross handle, at a more affordable cost, and at less risk of gaming losses.

There are always exceptions to this rule. Some properties cater to the "whale" or "high roller" table game player. However, even these properties have some form of slot player tracking system designed to build a database for marketing purposes. The Desert Inn in Las Vegas was a perfect example. The D.I. was an ultra deluxe property that offered golf and other first class amenities to high-end table game players, but it still had one of the best slot clubs in the industry. Casinos use the same criteria to develop a solid foundation for a Casino Marketing Department regardless of the market sought.

An absolute parallel exists in the operation of a Table Games Marketing Department and a Slot Marketing Department. In table games, we refer to the customers' marketing information as a "player list" but in the Slot Department we call this same marketing information a "database." They are, in many cases, the exact same players.

You can build your database of customers in the same way. Use a player tracking system, whether electronic card readers or a manual system, and use different criteria for each game or machine denomination to establish a net value of the player. The earning potential of each player will change based on the type of game they play. There are some very sophisticated formulas available, as well as more simplified ones. Whatever formula you use no matter what the customer plays, you still must establish a range of earning potential for each player. Use a similar system to evaluate the profitability of all of your various marketing activities directed to this player. This includes inviting the player as an individual or as a part of a group to your property for dinner, a special event, or a tournament. It still comes down to the basic definition of Casino Marketing: the ability to attract a qualified customer to a property at a cost that allows casinos to make a profit from their activities.

Slot Clubs

In the early 1980s, the competition, and large numbers of older, daily visitors to Atlantic City casinos caused the creation of the first "Slot Clubs." These first clubs were devised as a means to keep track of the customers who frequented their casinos as daily slot players, because the casinos wanted the ability to direct their marketing efforts to these individual players on a large scale, and to reward them for their continued loyalty. This marked a change from the "shot gun" slot marketing strategy to the "rifle shot" strategy.

The Sands and Harrah's Atlantic City were the early pioneers of the slot club. They modeled it after a system used by the airlines frequent flyer programs. As the gaming industry began to attract increasingly formally educated people, player-tracking systems became more sophisticated, and were built right into the machines, giving a more accurate picture of the individual slot customer's play. This basic premise has now expanded to all areas of the casino. The same concept, and in many cases the same system, is used in table games, baccarat, sports and race betting, and keno areas. Just about every casino in every gaming jurisdiction uses some sort of club or player tracking system in their marketing operation.

Several books have been written on the actual operating procedures of slot clubs and on the differences, both the positive and the negative aspects, of each club in relation to the customer and the casino. Casino executives should read these books. They provide a detailed and in-depth understanding of the various slot clubs. Slot manufacturers and the Systems Testing Laboratories publish additional valuable material on the specifics of player tracking systems. But, after you have this player database, remember you still must use it in conjunction with a sound Marketing Program.

CHAPTER 12: PREPARATION OF A YEARLY MARKETING PLAN

Chapter Outline

INTRODUCTION TO THE YEARLY MARKETING PLAN

The Board of Directors of Nick's Hotel and Casino has decided to accept your proposal to establish a Casino Marketing Department within their property. They were impressed with your marketing expertise and they have asked you to accept the position of Director of Casino Marketing. They have also requested that you coordinate the marketing efforts of the Hotel Sales Department, Room Reservations, and the Casino to coordinate the marketing efforts of an entire hotel/casino/resort property, it is necessary for all departments to understand the direction the property will take in its marketing efforts. This important task is usually accomplished through the coordinated efforts of all sales departments in the creation of a Yearly Marketing Plan. After gathering the pertinent property and marketing information from the Hotel Sales Manager, Advertising Manager and the Casino Manager, you are now prepared to coordinate this material into a Yearly Sales Marketing Plan for your property. This finished product is one of the most important reports prepared for your entire operation. When your Yearly Marketing Plan is complete, you will present it to the Board of Directors through the President/General Manager for their approval and then you will implement it.

NICK'S HOTEL AND CASINO
2002

MARKETING PLAN

INDEX

1. Nick's Hotel and Casino Marketing Philosophy
2. Economic Forecast
    a) International
    b) National
    c) Local
3. Competitive Activities
    a) International
    b) National
    c) Local
4. Analysis of Past Business
    a) General Market Statistical Analysis
    b) Narrative Analysis
    c) Casino Market Statistical Analysis
    d) Narrative Analysis
    e) Hotel Sales Statistical Analysis
    f) Narrative Analysis
    g) Room Reservations Statistical Analysis
    h) Narrative Analysis
5. Year 2000 Projected Marketing Mix
    a) Statistical Review of Each Market
    b) Narrative Summary
6. Year 2000 Projected Casino Handle and Complimentary Analysis
    a) Statistical Analysis
    b) Narrative Analysis
7. Advertising
8. Entertainment
9. Summary

MARKETING PHILOSOPHY
NICK'S HOTEL MARKETING PHILOSOPHY

In 2000, Nick's Hotel and Casino has a very aggressive marketing attitude by all members of its executive staff, especially by the members of the department charged with the responsibility of "selling" the property to our present and potential customers. We place emphasis on attracting casino-oriented customers to our hotel and casino, both as hotel guests, and visitors, when they are in town staying at a competitor's hotel. We have a Casino Marketing Department within our property that enables us to attack this highly competitive marketplace. Experience and contacts allow us to immediately compete in this field to attract casino customers and control related expenses.

The Hotel Sales Department places more emphasis on attracting higher quality tour and travel groups and small in-house conventions and incentive groups.

During 2000, we used all of our top executives to welcome the preferred travel agents and company representatives to our property to demonstrate that we value their business. The Sales Department also emphasizes the tour wholesale business because with a strong economy many people are seeking a discounted means of travel. However, we hope our need for this type of business will not be as great as it has been in the past, due to the aggressive emphasis that we put on sales efforts for casino business, high-quality tour and travel, and in-house convention business.

Our property is large enough (1,000 rooms) to offer all of the physical amenities necessary to make us competitive. Yet it is still small enough to extend a personal, friendly attitude to all of our guests, which is something our larger competitors cannot do and many of our smaller competitors are not willing to do. In summary, in 2000 Nick's Hotel and Casino is an aggressively and professionally managed property oriented to casino and preferred customers.

ECONOMIC FORECAST
INTERNATIONAL

At the present time, the countries of Western Europe are experiencing a strong economic period. All of the European countries are enjoying a very stable economy at this time but in relation to the U. S. dollar the Euro-dollar is down. This makes it a very good time for U.S. tourists to travel to Europe. European Countries recognize this opportunity, and have increased their efforts to attract the American tourist abroad. This may have an adverse effect on the tourist business to Las Vegas and other U.S. travel destinations. The unemployment rate is very low in Europe; consequently, more Europeans are traveling to the U.S. This somewhat offsets the imbalances of tourist travel.

The economy of Eastern Europe is still in shambles and is expected to remain this way for quite some time. This area does not offer a viable market for the U.S. travel industry to pursue.

The Japanese are making a comeback in most segments of their economy. The inroads they have made in the computer manufacturing industry and other electronic components have had a major impact on rebuilding and stabilizing their economy.

With the strengthening of the Japanese economy and the desire of the Japanese people to travel, Japan is still a good market for the U.S. resort industry to pursue.

The Mid-East market is still very unstable. These countries possess great wealth, but any marketing plans you have in this area must be directed to a relatively small number of individuals. Even then, you must take a very prudent stance when extending credit and clarify the method of payment prior to the start of casino play.

Mexico and parts of South America are still excellent marketplaces for the U. S. resort industry. The economy of Mexico continues to improve. Mexico still does not have legalized casinos and the short and easy travel time continues to make it a prime market for the U.S. gaming sites, especially Las Vegas. A major aspect to consider relative to the international marketplace is your ability to collect your accounts-receivable, and the danger of the fluctuating value of the currency of some countries.

NATIONAL

The economic climate of the U.S. is still very strong and continues to look exceptionally strong for the next several years. The Federal Banking Reserve, through the continued leadership of Mr. Greenspan, is very stable. He is satisfied that our growth rate is under control, and as a result, the increase in interest rates should not be a major economic factor for at least the next year or two. The inflation and unemployment rates are under control, as well. The average American household has more spendable income than ever, and as a result, the travel and gaming industry should enjoy banner years for at least the next 5 years.

The prime interest rate is expected to continue to be in the 7.5% to 8.5% for the foreseeable future. New housing sales are down only slightly but the housing market is still very strong. New car sales are up and continue to climb. Looking ahead, forecasters see a continued strong economy for the U.S. The only negative spot on the horizon that could adversely affect tourism, is the increased cost of fuel. This will make the cost of travel more expensive, especially by air.

LOCAL

The local economy will reflect the national economy to a very large degree, especially in the strength of our new home sales. Las Vegas is the fastest growing city in the United States. We have an average of 5000 new residents per month moving to Las Vegas. This has a major impact on all segments of our economy. The Las Vegas Valley now has over 1,000,000 permanent residents. Our new housing sales are higher than the national average, and our unemployment rate is lower than the national average. A very large percentage of the new residents are retired people with a steady, fixed income. This market has caused an economic boom for the local casino market, as is evidenced by the increased number of local establishments.

The tourist industry for the U.S. is very strong, with Las Vegas and Orlando leading the way as "Preferred Destinations." Las Vegas enjoys millions of visitors a year. This coupled with the increased local market indicates that Las Vegas will enjoy a very strong economy for many years to come.

COMPETITIVE ACTIVITIES
INTERNATIONAL

The strongest competition that we have in Europe for the American casino-oriented customer is Loew's Monte Carlo Hotel and Casino. It offers the most competition to U.S. casinos because it provides an opportunity for Americans to visit Europe "free" through a junket program and through the use of special casino promotions. The most successful promotion it offers is the Monte Carlo Grand Prix.

Casinos throughout England are not competition for U.S. casinos because Americans must wait 24 hours after arrival in England before they are permitted to gamble in the casinos. This regulation eliminates the use of junkets to attract Americans to those properties. The English casinos do not actively solicit American business. However, American casinos lose a great deal of Mid-Eastern and European business to the casinos in England as well as other casinos in France and Italy.

Aruba is operating a full junket program, and during the winter months it does a brisk business from the colder regions of the U.S. Aruba casinos also pay the junket representatives a commission based on their players' losses. This method of payment is very attractive to the representatives and consequently they "push" Aruba in the winter months. The casinos in the Caribbean and Central America have become more active in their marketing efforts, especially in the U.S. markets. Puerto Rico has launched a new marketing program in the U.S., as has the new Atlantis property in the Bahamas. Costa Rica enacted new gaming regulations that allow casinos to offer a larger variety of games and slot machines. As the casinos grow in size they will offer more amenities to U.S. players and will become stronger competition for U.S. casinos, especially those in the Southern States and portions of the East Coast.

NATIONAL

The biggest competition for Las Vegas now and even more so over the next several years is the continued legalization of casinos throughout the U.S., particularly tribal casinos. Gaming experts believe the growth of legal casinos in other jurisdictions has actually expanded the market of players, and as a result, more people are available and eager to come to Las Vegas. A review of growth statistics and visitor counts, confirms this theory. At some point, the industry has to level new player market growth. Larger gaming chains are now purchasing many smaller casino operations. Their marketing philosophy creates new customers, not only for their geographically local properties, but also to cross-market customers to their other properties as well.

The major concern at this time is the impact of the new gaming regulations in California. This new regulation allows Las Vegas-style gaming at tribal casinos, including slot machines. Since California has always been such a strong market for us, there is concern whether or not we can attract more players to expand the market faster than we will lose them to local California casinos.

LOCAL

Most properties in Las Vegas have attempted to increase their base of casino-oriented customers through the use of Casino Hosts and major special events. These strategies will bring additional patrons into casinos. However, casinos that control expenses when "buying" business will realize the greatest net profit.

Smaller properties need to take advantage of the major promotions hosted by larger hotels and to also look for opportunities to participate in charity events or national sporting events. By participating in these types of events, they can attract customers to their properties without having the heavy expenses of hosting a special event.

The most important element to the success of our Marketing Program in the future is to make sure all levels of our personnel make our customers feel welcome. The near future will be profitable for most of the Las Vegas properties due to the strength of the national and local economy.

The Las Vegas Convention Authority is one of the best in the world. They will continue to excel in marketing Las Vegas, especially to major conventions. The new, mega-resorts in Las Vegas will benefit from this ever-increasing convention business, especially those with their own convention space. However, now is the time to plan for the future by creating a strong, profitable Casino Marketing Office and operation.

ANALYSIS OF PAST BUSINESS
NARRATIVE ANALYSIS OF PAST BUSINESS
GENERAL – 2001

In 2001 the average monthly occupancy rate was 90%, an acceptable level of occupancy considering the average occupancy level in Las Vegas for major hotels is only 86% and the national average is 67%.

The problem with our occupancy level was not the overall number of rooms occupied, but the quality of our Marketing Mix. The casino used only 15% of the available rooms. The overall occupancy level also suffered. The reservations made by the Room Reservations Department accounted for only 31%. This means that we did not attract enough individual business. Fortunately, the Sales Department brought in business during the weaker summer months. The low occupancy by the Room Reservations Department and the casino, especially in the summer months, demonstrates a lack of proper planning and coordination between the Sales Department and the Advertising Department. The lack of individual business our hotel attracted all year confirmed this theory.

An individual analysis of each Sales Department follows.

Figure 12.1 Nick's Hotel and Casino – 2001 – General Marketing Analysis

MONTH*	CASINO		SALES		ROOM RESERVATIONS		TOTAL ROOM NIGHTS	OCCUPANCY %
	ROOM NIGHTS	%	ROOM NIGHTS	%	ROOM NIGHTS	%		
JANUARY	4500	15	12000	40	10500	35	27000	90
FEBRUARY (28 DAYS)	4760	17	12600	45	8680	31	26040	93
MARCH	5400	18	12600	42	9900	33	27900	93
APRIL	4500	15	12000	40	11100	37	27600	92
MAY	4800	16	12600	42	9900	33	27300	91
JUNE	3000	10	15300	51	6300	21	24600	82
JULY	3000	10	15900	53	6600	22	25500	85
AUGUST	3000	10	16500	55	7200	24	26700	89
SEPTEMBER	5100	17	13500	45	9900	33	28500	95
OCTOBER	5400	18	12600	42	10500	35	28500	95
NOVEMBER	4800	16	12300	41	11700	39	28800	96
DECEMBER	6600	22	9600	32	7200	24	23400	78
YEARLY AVERAGE	15%		44%		31%			90%

* All months for these examples are based on 30 days, except February

NARRATIVE ANALYSIS OF PAST CASINO BUSINESS
CASINO

In the recent past, the casino used an average of only 15% of the available rooms. This low room usage by the casino created an average just $800 per occupied room in casino handle. The junkets only produced an average of 5% usage of the available rooms. In the near future, this figure should be brought to the 8% level. The main reason junkets averaged only 5% is because we neither encouraged nor supported the junket representatives in sending individual splinters to the hotel/casino, nor did we invite them to participate in our special events.

The special events were right on target at 1% per month, but the only reason was the outstanding success we had with the Super Bowl promotion in January and the success in December with the Anniversary Party and the New Year's Party.

The Invited Guests only averaged 7%. To increase this to our desired 10% level, we must hire at least three additional experienced Casino Hosts. The casino-rated rooms averaged close to 2%, which is too high. We must reduce it to the 1% level. In summary, our Casino Marketing efforts are only slightly below the desired level. With a little more aggressive planning and implementation, we will reach our goal of 20% room usage by the casino.

Figure 12.2 Statistical Analysis of Past Business - Casino 2001

MONTH	JUNKETS		SPECIAL EVENTS		INVITED GUESTS		CASINO RATE		TOTAL	% OF OCCUPANCY
	Room Nights	%	Room Nights	%	Room Nights	%	Room Nights	%	Room Nights	
JANUARY	1500	5	900	3	1500	5	600	2	4500	15
FEBRUARY	1680	6	---	---	2800	10	280	1	4760	17
MARCH	2700	9	300	1	2100	7	300	1	5400	18
APRIL	2100	7	---	---	2100	7	300	1	4500	15
MAY	1800	6	---	---	2400	8	600	2	4800	16
JUNE	900	3	---	---	1500	5	600	2	3000	10
JULY	900	3	600	2	1200	4	300	1	3000	10
AUGUST	1200	4	---	---	1500	5	300	1	3000	10
SEPTEMBER	1500	5	---	---	3000	10	600	2	5100	17
OCTOBER	2100	7	600	2	2100	7	600	2	5400	18
NOVEMBER	2100	7	---	---	2100	7	600	2	4800	16
DECEMBER	600	2	2400	8	3000	10	600	2	6600	22
AVERAGE	5%		1%		7%		2%			15%

NARRATIVE ANALYSIS OF PAST BUSINESS
    SALES DEPARTMENT
    In the recent past Sales Department personnel did an excellent job in providing this property with occupants for our rooms. They achieved an average occupancy of available rooms of 44%.
    However, an analysis of their mix of business, revealed that their efforts (and results) were misdirected. They concentrated on business from the Travel Agents and, as a result, achieved a disproportionate mix of business. A closer examination of the large amount of business from this source in the summer months, clearly showed that they realized they were facing a lower occupancy in the weaker summer months, and, consequently, dropped their room rates in a panic to attract this segment of the market. The abilities of the personnel must be examined to determine if we have enough qualified salespeople who "sell" our property to corporate executives for in-house conventions and incentive groups. If we improve these two areas, we can reduce the number of rooms we allocate to citywide conventions and to the tour wholesalers. We must also perform an in-depth analysis of the coordination of the advertising program and the Sales Department to ensure that we advertise in the necessary places so we can achieve our desired Marketing Mix. In summary, we have a competent, hard working sales force, but the direction of their efforts must be concentrated more on the in-house conventions and incentive groups market.

Figure 12.3 Statistical Analysis of Past Business --Sales Department – 2001

MONTH	CITY WIDE CONVENTIONS		IN-HOUSE CONVENTIONS		INCENTIVE GROUPS		TOUR AND TRAVEL		TOUR WHOLESALE		TOTAL	
	ROOM NIGHTS	%	ROOM NIGHTS	%	ROOM NIGHTS	%	ROOM NIGHTS	%	ROOM NIGHTS	%	ROOM NIGHTS	%
JAN	6000	20	--	--	--	--	3000	10	3000	10	12000	40
FEB	--	--	3000	10	4500	15	2700	9	3300	11	12600	45
MAR	2700	9	2100	7	1500	5	3000	10	3300	11	12600	42
APR	2700	9	1500	5	1800	6	3000	10	3000	10	12000	40
MAY	1200	4	3000	10	1800	6	3300	11	3300	11	12600	42
JUNE	3000	10	600	2	300	1	6600	22	4800	16	15300	51
JULY	1500	5	1200	4	600	2	7200	24	5400	18	15900	53
AUG	2400	8	600	2	900	3	6600	22	6000	20	16500	55
SEPT	900	3	900	3	3000	10	4800	16	3900	13	13500	45
OCT	1200	4	900	3	3300	11	3900	13	3300	11	12600	42
NOV	1500	5	1500	5	3000	10	3000	10	3300	11	12300	41
DEC	1500	5	2100	7	300	1	3600	12	2100	7	9600	32
AVE	7%		5%		6%		14%		12%		44%	

NARRATIVE ANALYSIS OF PAST BUSINESS
ROOM RESERVATIONS

In the past, the Room Reservations Department did not fill enough rooms for our property. The reservations made by individual customers accounted for only 19% occupancy of our available rooms. This area should have been at the 30% level. When individual reservations account for only 19% of our overall occupancy, it indicates that we need more advertising directed to this market. The clerks who take calls from people inquiring about reservations are not properly handling these calls and/or are not "closing" the sale by making the reservation.

The individual packages accounted for an average occupancy of 7%, approximately 2% above the 5% level we would like to have from this area. This happened because our Sales Department directed most of its sales efforts to travel agents. The strong package sales of 10% in December confirms this point. The Sales Department sold a special reduced rate December package. We do not want to lose our rapport with the travel agents. We want to improve our contacts in other areas.

The walk-in customers use an average of 5% of the available rooms. This is exactly the level that we want in this area of our business. This tells us that we are attracting customers to our property after they arrive in town. To accomplish this, our hotel/casino must have a good reputation, and our billboards and other advertising directed toward this market does an effective job. This level of walk-in business also validates that our desk clerks are doing a good job of "selling" our property to prospective customers when they come in to inquire about a room. In summary, we should reduce the number of individual packages we sell, and redesign our sales efforts to the individual customer market.

Figure 12.4 Statistical Analysis of Past Business-- Room Reservations – 2001

MONTH	INDIVIDUALS		PACKAGES		WALK-INS		TOTAL	
	ROOM NIGHTS	%	ROOM NIGHTS	%	ROOM NIGHTS	%	ROOM NIGHTS	%
JANUARY	7500	25	1200	4	1800	6	10500	35
FEBRUARY	5400	18	1800	6	2100	7	8680	31
MARCH	6300	21	1800	6	1800	6	9900	33
APRIL	7200	24	2100	7	1800	6	11100	37
MAY	6300	21	2100	7	1500	5	9900	33
JUNE	2700	9	2400	8	1200	4	6300	21
JULY	3000	10	2400	8	1200	4	6600	22
AUGUST	3000	10	2700	9	1500	5	7200	24
SEPTEMBER	7500	25	1500	5	900	3	9900	33
OCTOBER	7200	24	2100	7	1200	4	10500	35
NOVEMBER	6900	23	2400	8	2400	8	11700	39
DECEMBER	3000	10	3000	10	1200	4	7200	24
AVERAGE	19%		7%		5%		31%	

2000 MARKETING MIX
NARRATIVE ANALYSIS

In the future, our general Marketing Mix should improve in both quality and quantity. More emphasis will be placed on our efforts to attract casino customers to our property because we will establish a Casino Marketing Office. Our Sales Department will put more emphasis on selling our property to corporations to use as a convention center for incentive group meetings and in-house conventions.

This year we intended to reduce the number of rooms we use for the lower-rated markets, the wholesale tour market, and to the package customers. However, until we redirect our advertising program so that it will attract the individual customer to our property, we must use these two markets as occupancy fillers. Our Sales Department will continue to work closely with the travel agents because we need their help in the summer months and in December.

Figure 12.5 2002 Marketing Mix

MONTH	CASINO		SALES DEPARTMENT		ROOM RESERVATIONS		TOTAL ROOM NIGHTS	% of OCCU-PANCY
	Room Nights	%	Room Nights	%	Room Nights	%		
JANUARY	7500	25	18000	60	4500	15	30000	100
FEBRUARY (28 DAYS)	6160	22	11200	40	8400	30	25760	92
MARCH	6000	20	12000	40	10500	35	28500	95
APRIL	6000	20	13500	45	7500	25	27000	90
MAY	6000	20	12000	40	11400	38	29400	98
JUNE	4500	15	13500	45	10500	35	28500	95
JULY	4500	15	13500	45	10500	35	28500	95
AUGUST	4500	15	13500	45	10500	35	28500	95
SEPTEMBER	6600	22	12000	40	9000	30	27600	92
OCTOBER	6000	20	12000	40	9000	30	27600	92
NOVEMBER	6000	20	12000	40	9000	30	27600	92
DECEMBER	7500	25	10500	35	7500	25	25500	85
AVERAGE	20%		43%		30%		93%	

Figure 12.6 2002 Casino Marketing Mix

MONTH	JUNKETS		SPECIAL EVENTS		INVITED GUESTS		CASINO RATE		TOTAL	
	Room Nights	%	Room Nights	%	Room Nights	%	Room Nights	%	Room Nights	Percentage
JANUARY	1500	5	1500	5	3600	12	900	3	7500	25
FEBRUARY 28 DAYS	2800	10	1400	5	1680	6	280	1	6160	22
MARCH	3000	10	---	---	2700	9	300	1	6000	20
APRIL	3000	10	---	---	2700	9	300	1	6000	20
MAY	2400	8	1500	5	1800	6	300	1	6000	20
JUNE	2100	7	150	.5	1650	5.5	600	2	4500	15
JULY	2100	7	300	1	1500	5	600	2	4500	15
AUGUST	2100	7	150	.5	1650	5.5	600	2	4500	15
SEPTEMBER	3000	10	900	3	2400	8	300	1	6600	22
OCTOBER	3000	10	---	---	2700	9	300	1	6000	20
NOVEMBER	3000	10	---	---	2700	9	300	1	6000	20
DECEMBER	2400	8	1800	6	3000	10	600	2	7500	25
TOTAL	8.5%		2%		8%		1.5%		20%	

Figure 12.7 2002 Sales Department Marketing Mix

MONTH	CITY WIDE CONVENTIONS		IN-HOUSE CONVENTIONS		INCENTIVE GROUPS		TOUR AND TRAVEL		TOUR WHOLESALERS		TOTAL	
	ROOM NIGHTS	%	ROOM NIGHTS	%	ROOM NIGHTS	%	ROOM NIGHTS	%	ROOM NIGHTS	%	ROOM NIGHTS	%
JAN	9000	30	--	--	1500	5	4500	15	3000	10	18000	60
FEB	560	2	2800	10	2800	10	2800	10	2240	8	11200	40
MAR	1500	5	1500	5	3600	12	3000	10	2400	8	12000	40
APR	1500	5	3000	10	4500	15	2400	8	2100	7	13500	45
MAY	1500	5	2400	8	4800	16	1500	5	1800	6	12000	40
JUNE	3000	10	3000	10	3000	10	3000	10	1500	5	13500	45
JULY	3000	10	3000	10	3000	10	3000	10	1500	5	13500	45
AUG	3000	10	3000	10	3000	10	3000	10	1500	5	13500	45
SEPT	1500	5	900	3	6000	20	2100	7	1500	5	12000	40
OCT	600	2	2400	8	6000	20	1500	5	1500	5	12000	40
NOV	600	2	3900	13	4500	15	1500	5	1500	5	12000	40
DEC	900	3	1800	6	2400	8	3000	10	2400	8	10500	35
AVERAGE	7.4%		7.8%		12.6%		8.8%		6.4%		43%	

Figure 12.8 2002 Room Reservations Marketing Mix

MONTH	INDIVIDUALS		PACKAGES		WALK-INS		TOTAL	
	ROOM NIGHTS	%	ROOM NIGHTS	%	ROOM NIGHTS	%	ROOM NIGHTS	%
JANUARY	4200	14	---	---	300	1	4500	15
FEBRUARY	5600	20	1400	5	1400	5	8400	30
MARCH	7500	25	1500	5	1500	5	10500	35
APRIL	3900	13	2100	7	1500	5	7500	25
MAY	7500	25	1500	5	2400	8	11400	38
JUNE	6000	20	2400	8	2100	7	10500	35
JULY	6000	20	2400	8	2100	7	10500	35
AUGUST	6000	20	2400	8	2100	7	10500	35
SEPTEMBER	6000	20	1500	5	1500	5	9000	30
OCTOBER	6000	20	1500	5	1500	5	9000	30
NOVEMBER	6000	20	1500	5	1500	5	9000	30
DECEMBER	3000	10	3000	10	1500	5	7500	25
AVERAGE	19%		6%		5%		30%	

FUTURE PROJECTED CASINO HANDLE AND COMPLIMENTARY ANALYSIS

ANALYSIS

In the future, we should hold our expenditures in each area for complimentary airfare, room, and food and beverage to the 4% level. This will only be done if we evaluate the casino activities of all players we bring to our casino and extend complimentary privileges based on their value to our property. We must remain frugal when extending complimentary airfare because this area represents direct cash payments to the player. We must not reimburse airfare to customers who owe money. We should deduct this amount from their outstanding markers. In the months that our casino occupancy exceeds the 20% level of available rooms, we should average over $1,000 in casino handle per occupied room. In the slower summer months, we should still handle $800 in the casino for every occupied room. A large degree of our success will depend how we control the "cost" of our business.

Figure 12.9 2002 Casino Handle and Complimentary Analysis

MONTH	ROOM NIGHTS	CASINO HANDLE PER ROOM NIGHT ($)	ESTIMATED CASINO HANDLE ($)	AIRFARE TO CASINO HANDLE		RFB TO CASINO HANDLE	
				%	$	%	$
JANUARY	30000	1000	30000000	5	1500000	4	1200000
FEBRUARY	25760	1000	25760000	4	1030400	4	1030400
MARCH	28500	950	27075000	4	1083000	4	1083000
APRIL	27000	950	25650000	4	1026000	4	1026000
MAY	29400	950	27930000	4	1117200	4	1117200
JUNE	28500	800	22800000	3	684000	3	684000
JULY	28500	800	22800000	3	684000	3	684000
AUGUST	28500	800	22800000	3	684000	3	684000
SEPTEMBER	27600	1000	27600000	4	1104000	4	1104000
OCTOBER	27600	950	26220000	4	1048800	4	1048800
NOVEMBER	27600	950	26220000	4	1048800	4	1048800
DECEMBER	25500	1000	25500000	5	1275000	5	1275000
TOTAL	334460	928	310355000	4%	12285000	4	11985200

ADVERTISING

In the future, we will change the direction of our advertising program. Last year, we spent a major portion of our budget advertising our showroom locally and in the travel agent market. This year we will put more emphasis on attracting the individual customer to our property, and we will attempt to establish a more defined image of our property with more consistency in our advertising. We will use more printed media aimed at the general consumer and we will use television and radio, but on a regional and national level rather than locally. The consistency in our ads, both printed and air-media, will make our property more identifiable to the general public. The Director of Advertising in the near future will submit a detailed budget and media breakdown.

ENTERTAINMENT

At the present time, our main showroom policy is that of the "superstar" headliner. Last year, we had excellent attendance and because of this, we generated additional casino play from customers other than those who stayed in our hotel. An analysis of the revenue from our showroom indicates that currently, we are generating enough income to offset the cost of the entertainment in the room.

However, if the trend of ever-increasing costs for the "superstars" continues, we must be prepared to find an alternate mode of entertainment for our guests. We have two immediate alternatives available to us. We could put a production show in our room or we could expand our lounge entertainment. The Entertainment Director is preparing a feasibility study of these two alternatives and a complete showroom schedule and budget.

SUMMARY

In the future we will market ourselves more aggressively than in the past. We will put more emphasis on attracting casino-oriented customers to our property through the creation of a Casino Marketing Office. Our Sales Department will also stress attracting a more lucrative customer to our property. They will address the potential of the corporate market in the hope of bringing in-house conventions and incentive groups to our hotel. The Advertising Department will strive to establish an identifiable image for us. This will make our hotel more attractive to the individual customer market.

In general, we will upgrade the quality of guests we have at our property. At the same time, we will institute a system to evaluate the value of these customers to our bottom-line, to better control our cost of sales in the marketplace.

INDEX